Work
Wife

Work Wife

The Power of Female Friendship to Drive Successful Businesses

ERICA CERULO AND CLAIRE MAZUR

Ballantine Books
New York

Published in the United States by Ballantine Books, an imprint of
Random House, a division of Penguin Random House LLC, New York.

BALLANTINE and the HOUSE colophon are registered trademarks of
Penguin Random House LLC.

LIBRARY OF CONGRESS CATALOGING-IN-PUBLICATION DATA
Names: Cerulo, Erica, author. | Mazur, Claire, author.
Title: Work wife : the power of female friendship to drive
successful businesses / Erica Cerulo and Claire Mazur.
Description: New York : Ballantine Books, [2019]
Identifiers: LCCN 2018051136 | ISBN 9781524796778 (hardcover)
Subjects: LCSH: Businesswomen. | Women-owned business enterprises. |
Female friendship. | Partnership. | Success in business.
Classification: LCC HD6054.3 .C445 2019 | DDC 658.4/09082—dc23
LC record available at https://lccn.loc.gov/2018051136

Printed in the United States of America on acid-free paper

randomhousebooks.com

987654321

First Edition

Book design by Debbie Glasserman

TO EACH OTHER, AS CHEESY AS THAT SOUNDS

Contents

Work
Wife

Taking a Wife

Sometimes I get concerned about being a career woman. I get to thinking my job is too important to me. And I tell myself that the people I work with are just the people I work with and not my family. And last night I thought, "What is a family, anyway?" They're just people who make you feel less alone and really loved.

—MARY RICHARDS, *THE MARY TYLER MOORE SHOW*

About a year after we cofounded our company, Of a Kind, just as we were getting our businesswoman bearings, we sat in our office with a male professional acquaintance discussing a project we've long since forgotten. What we do recall is that the previous tenants had painted the walls a truly insane shade of brown, but we were too busy to remedy it and proud to have a space of our own nonetheless. Similarly burned in our memories: the moment that abruptly marked the end of that meeting, when the man across the table said, "Oh, I get it. You're the smart one, and you're the pretty one,"

nodding toward each of us in turn. We reacted to his degrada-
tion with stunned silence. What we *should* have said in response
was, "No, we're both smart, we're both pretty—immaterial as
that is—and, as long as we're sharing bios, we're both driven,
compassionate, savvy, and, frankly, pretty fucking funny, too."
Those are the reasons we chose each other, first as friends in
2002 and later as business partners in 2010, and why moments
like this bond us instead of break us.

   Our friendship started on the campus of the University of
Chicago, where we'd been set up on a friend date based on one
very silly thing: Claire, a freshman a scant few months into
the school year, had begun dating a basketball player . . . and
Erica, a sophomore, had dated a basketball player *her* freshman year, too. A coincidence like this was not to be overlooked; the opportunity for Erica to impart hard-earned
wisdom on the topic could not be passed up. We both greeted
the suggestion that we should meet on the basis of aligned
dating decisions with the exaggerated eye roll perfected by
eighteen- and nineteen-year-old women worldwide. But—no
spoilers here—we ended up really liking each other. Sitting
face-to-face at lunch in the fancy dining hall, with Harry Pot-
teresque vaulted ceilings towering above stir-fry stations, we
bonded hard and fast—over shopping, musicals, and growing
up the only Jewish (emphasis on the *ish*) one in our friend set.
Erica recalls thinking that the Hello Kitty calendar hanging in
Claire's dorm room felt like a very good sign. Claire remembers being intrigued by Erica's steadfast commitment to a
wardrobe of exclusively black, white, and pink. From these

tiny sparks of mutual admiration, we developed a connection. But it was one that felt uncommon for college-age women: We didn't traipse around the quad together with a half dozen others. At its core, our friendship was built for two.

We both moved to New York City after graduating, armed with plans to take over the magazine world (Erica) and the art world (Claire). Fast-forward to a job search in January 2010 when Claire's request for Erica's feedback on a cover letter spun out into a sprawling email chain that culminated in an idea for an online business—one that spoke to passions we'd nurtured independently in our careers and together as friends. The founding concept for Of a Kind, refined over lengthy IM sessions and stolen lunch breaks at now-shuttered coffee shops, was to commission emerging fashion designers to create limited-edition pieces that we'd release for sale in conjunction with stories about the makers behind them—their inspirations, their processes, the things that made them tick. In treating what we were selling with so much care and context, we hoped to encourage a sense of conscious consumption around fashion. We wanted to introduce a mentality of collecting, not just consuming, and to expose our audience to the thrill that comes with connecting on a human level to the work and the story of a designer. That summer, we quit our jobs, and in November, we launched a website.

When we started our company in 2010, we were eight years into our friendship. Since then, we've ticked off plenty of entrepreneurial milestones: moving into our first office space, making our first hire, securing our first big-deal partnership.

Over time, our business grew beyond our initial concept to reflect both of our expanding interests. We launched new product categories, including home, personal care, and paper goods. And as our business evolved, so did our understanding that what worked about Of a Kind was not just the products, but also our enthusiasm for sharing them and the way our relationship brought that out in each other. We'd always been transparent with our customers about who we were and what our lives looked like (early customer service emails were signed "Claire + Erica" because we were, in fact, the ones writing them), and our audience responded in turn with feedback that Of a Kind felt like a trusted friend . . . that just happened to be a store on the internet.

That comparison was a real point of pride for us, and we kept it front-of-mind as we took the business in new directions: In 2012, we launched a weekly newsletter called "10 Things," which is not so far off from the kind of email a pal might send sharing a very random smattering of discoveries ranging from snacks to face serums, novels to running shoes. As it developed a cultish following, we launched a podcast, A Few Things, which follows a similar premise but has the added value of putting our chemistry on (sonic) display. Today, we describe Of a Kind as "giving our best discoveries the audience they deserve," and we describe ourselves and our customers as "Professional Enthusiasts"—a term we've printed (artfully, of course) on sweatshirts, hats, and all manner of stylish merch.

Along the way, a lot has gone on behind the scenes: Our

team has grown and shrunk and grown again, we've moved offices, our roles have changed, and we even sold the business—to everyone's favorite place to go to buy one thing but leave with nine, Bed Bath & Beyond. We still run the show—albeit with a parent company—and even with all the shifting, we're still the two of us, this many years in.

When asked about our proudest business accomplishment, the answer is always "Us!"—the friendship we've nurtured and the successful partnership it's fostered. What we've realized in taking a closer look at the ways in which our relationship functions is that our professional partnership has been the beneficiary of the tenets that anchor female friendship: emotional intimacy, vulnerability, a penchant for collaboration, and a pattern of mutual support—qualities that have unique power and potential to spawn great ideas and create foundations for strong businesses.

In making the transition from friends to business partners all those years ago, we knew we were signing up for a much more complex relationship. We went from seeing each other weekly to spending more time together than we did sleeping. Finances became a constant topic of conversation, and not just in the context of whether one of us was feeling too broke for a dinner date. We spent our nights, weekends, and soon 9-to-5s each making decisions that would affect the other. Our careers and our futures became intertwined.

Though this transformation felt natural to us—how else would someone do something as scary as start a business other than with a close friend by their side?—we encountered plenty of people whose eyes popped out of their heads when we told them we were taking our personal relationship professional. Oh, the horror stories! The whole plot of *The Social Network*! Sure, we recognized that in pursuing this at all, we could be putting our friendship on the line. But our shared history brought us immense, intense comfort—a much-sought-after feeling during the constant turbulence and uncertainty that come with building something from the ground up. We also walked into this knowing we saw each other as equals; there was no power dynamic to contend with, and we trusted that would remain a constant. At some point, after enough soul-crushing investor meetings and awkward interviews with job candidates, the looming sense that we could walk out of this venture short a business *and* a bud faded away. Once we'd put enough hours, years, and life into Of a Kind, it was clear that if something didn't work out with the business, our relationship would survive, just as it had plenty of other lows. We were in this together, even if "this" ceased to exist. Though a certain—mostly male—breed of human loves to pit women against one another, as if every female duo is Brenda and Kelly on the matching-formal-dress episode of *Beverly Hills 90210,* proving those people wrong—both in friendship and in business—has been a career highlight.

We are hardly the only women who've found something appealing about pairing up: While prepping to have new headshots taken, as we do and dread annually, we turned to the internet for inspiration/instruction on how to pose without looking like Mary-Kate and Ashley Olsen on the poster for *Two of a Kind: How to Flunk Your First Date*. It was there, in our Google Images search results, that we realized how many of the new ventures taking over the world were run by pairs of women: Elizabeth Cutler & Julie Rice of SoulCycle (who, in photos, benefit unfairly from the use of bikes as props), Betsy Beers & Shonda Rhimes of Shondaland (who have taken the Olsen approach), Phoebe Robinson & Jessica Williams of 2 Dope Queens (who excel at giving don't-mess-with-us face), Dr. Katie Rodan & Dr. Kathy Fields of Rodan + Fields (who love a crossed-arm power pose). Whereas ten years prior our vision board of high-profile business partnerships likely would have been littered with awkward snapshots of men who'd monopolized the space—Jobs and Wozniak, Gates and Allen, Procter and Gamble, Ben and Jerry—we now had plenty of female icons to reference. (And to thank for surfacing posing options beyond huddling together seriously—but passionately—over a computer or a pint of Chunky Monkey.)

This shift isn't a coincidence—it's a direct consequence of an evolving business environment. Slow but steady progress toward dismantling male dominance at the office has carved out space for women to collaborate instead of compete professionally, and that's set the stage for change. As we'll explore over the next eight chapters, duos and trios of women who have partnered in leadership positions are paving the way for a reimagined workplace that leads with qualities like compassion, mutual support, and transparency. They're implementing long-view practices that result in strong business outcomes. These partnerships are changing not just what it means to be women in the workplace, but the workplace as a whole.

In the pages that follow, we'll look to our own story and the stories of other game-changing women collaborators— from financiers to Olympians to cannabis entrepreneurs—to better understand and explain this transformation. We'll dive into the micro: How do women partners talk about money, delegate, scale, hire, fire, cope with burnout, and still hug it out at the end of the day? And we'll explore the macro—the ways in which work wives are prioritizing vulnerability and openness in the C-suite and improving workplaces to better accommodate and support women, parents, and others disadvantaged by outdated patriarchal business conventions.

This evolution in the business world coincides, unsurprisingly, with a long-overdue cultural shift that recognizes that female friendships aren't all about backstabbing and cattiness. The *Mean Girls* narrative got hit by a bus and in its wake came #squadgoals and Shine Theory—the former being a sentiment of solidarity that originated with Gucci Mane and Waka Flocka Flame before being co-opted by Taylor Swift and the whole internet, and the latter being a philosophy developed by Ann Friedman and Aminatou Sow (more from them in the upcoming chapters) that's rooted in the idea that we ought to befriend, not compete with, women we admire. Since emerging on the scene in 2013, Shine Theory has spread like wildfire.

Naturally, this ethos also holds true for friendships at the office. The age of the underminery Tess McGill/Katharine Parker *Working Girl* rivalry is behind us, and Oprah and Gayle, Abbi and Ilana, Kathie Lee and Hoda, and Tina and Amy are the new relationship role models. "Work wife," a term spawned from "office wife"—which itself dates back to the 1930s, when it was used by men to describe an especially high-functioning secretary—is taking on new meaning in our current era. Its connotation has evolved just as office culture and marriage have, and more recently it's been adopted to describe a combination of personal and professional bondedness and healthy, supportive closeness among women. It's a dynamic that requires an in-this-together attitude and approach that's viable in any business setting with right-minded people.

In 2013, the National Bureau of Economic Research embarked on a study to answer the question "Are Women More Attracted to Cooperation Than Men?" and the quick answer was "Yup." To speak, for a moment, in sweeping generalizations: This study suggests women do worse in competitive environments and better when part of a team. And unlike men, who, the same research shows, tend to prefer to work alone, women *like* collaborating. Numerous studies suggest that this inclination is in line with how we're socialized: Men are brought up to be more competitive, independent, and unemotional, while women are raised to be more supportive, cooperative, and emotionally sensitive. In turn, that informs what we look for when it comes to friendship—women bond by sharing feelings, not just activities, which is how men tend to engage and sustain friendships. And shared feelings can lead to a hell of a business proposition. Nicole Kidman, in her Emmy acceptance for her performance in *Big Little Lies,* the hit HBO miniseries she produced and starred in with Reese Witherspoon, summed up this idea succinctly: "This is a friendship that then created opportunities. It created opportunities out of a frustration, because we weren't getting offered great roles."

The unfortunate fact of the matter is that as women we have a rougher go of it in the workplace—whether on a Hollywood set or in a cubicle—and, for all of the camaraderie and mind-melding benefits, being part of a pair also serves as a defense mechanism. Being able to turn to someone and say "Am I crazy?" is a boon because women are made to question their own sanity all the time. Female hysteria may no longer be recognized as a medical condition, but the stereotype—and the reliance on it as a tool to silence and discredit women—persists. Having someone to validate perceptions helps eradicate the self-doubt that can rattle even the most confident among us.

Take, as some very unsettling proof, the #MeToo sexual harassment and assault reckoning of 2017, which was facilitated in part by the comfort accusers took in coming forward alongside other women instead of alone, and the entire activist movement that coalesced around it—an undeniable testament to the power of women partnering and a rock-solid case for work-wifing if there ever was one. The Harvey Weinstein story—brought to us by the *New York Times* reporters (and work wives?) Jodi Kantor and Megan Twohey—and all those that followed in its wake were a reinforcement of what we already knew to be true, writ large: The traditional workplace wasn't designed for women. Claiming our rightful places in it requires resetting priorities and rewriting rules. The way we see it, the most effective way to do that is by honoring the strength of the bonds that exist between women and using that as fuel for change.

This book is meant to show—and to celebrate—how some women have done this, but not to assert that there is *one* way to do it. Although all of the collaborators we interviewed are or were in leadership positions and many are entrepreneurs who helm the companies they started, this is not meant to suggest that either is a prerequisite to work-wifing. But what we *have* found is that the style of partnership we're making a case for is, for the time being, much easier to actualize in entrepreneurial environments where leaders are blazing their own trails. While more traditional corporate structures may accommodate and encourage teamwork, they typically evaluate people on the basis of their individual contributions instead of as pairs or groups (promotions, for example, are rarely awarded in tandem). As more women—and more work wives—ascend the ranks, though, corporate norms will shift to embrace all sorts of traditionally feminine traits, collaboration among them.

And speaking of feminine traits: We rely on them to make our case, but that's not intended to disregard that claiming anything as inherently feminine is a loaded and at times problematic act. In a culture where we've come to acknowledge that biology does not determine gender, claiming that it somehow determines personality may seem at best outdated and at worst discriminatory. Class, race, age, ability, and the advantages and privileges, or lack thereof, that attend them add another layer of complexity. For our purposes, we're looking at feminine traits—and the friendships that follow from them—as reflections of how most women in the United States and the Western world at large have been socialized, by way of their upbringing, the media, or social norms. Our definition of "woman" includes anyone who identifies as such. Gender stereotypes and expectations can be constricting, exhausting, and disempowering; rather than reinforcing them, we hope to better understand the ways in which they inform us—specifically in our relationships and in our work—and to use that understanding to effect change and progress for everyone.

We hope that what follows spreads the joy that we've experienced in taking our friendship professional, enough to inspire others to do it, too. In proclaiming and championing the power of female partnerships in the workplace, we aim to expedite a transformation already under way. That means friends bringing business into the fold, businesses bringing friendship into the fold, or, best of all, both.

In writing this book, we wanted to look beyond our own partnership—our professional dynamic and the friendship that anchors it—in order to better understand what makes women work well together. In doing so, we also wanted to share and to celebrate the experiences of other duos and trios who've chosen to put work-wifing at the core of their careers. The pages that follow are filled with their stories and insights, revealing their chemistry in action and underscoring the authenticity that they bring to their partnerships. Ahead are the quick-and-dirty facts about them (along with photos, that, hey, might even provide a little posing inspiration).

JAMIE BECK

ERICA CERULO AND CLAIRE MAZUR (US!)

/

First meeting

In the dining hall at the University of Chicago in 2002

Partners since

2010

Location

Brooklyn, New York

Work-wife undertaking

The small-maker-centric ecommerce website Of a Kind and,
well, this book you're reading.

Pictured: Erica (left) and Claire

DESCRIBE THE FAUNA

GINA DELVAC, ANN FRIEDMAN, AND AMINATOU SOW
/

First meeting

Aminatou & Ann at a *Gossip Girl* viewing party in 2008; Ann & Gina through a
mutual friend in 2011; Gina & Aminatou on a women's desert retreat in 2013

Partners since

2014

Location

Los Angeles, California (Gina & Ann), and Brooklyn, New York (Aminatou)

Work-wife undertaking

The cultish podcast Call Your Girlfriend

Pictured from left: Ann, Gina, and Aminatou

JAMES RANSOM

AMANDA HESSER AND MERRILL STUBBS

/

First meeting

Working together on *The Essential New York Times Cookbook* in 2004

Partners since

2009

Location

New York, New York

Work-wife undertaking

The kitchen and home destination Food52

Pictured: Merrill (left) and Amanda

SASHA ISRAEL

KATHRYN AND ELIZABETH "LIZZIE" FORTUNATO

First meeting

In utero in 1984—they're twins!

Partners since

2008

Location

New York, New York

Work-wife undertaking

The jewelry and accessories line Lizzie Fortunato

Pictured: Kathryn (left) and Lizzie

KIM FRANCE AND ANDREA LINETT

First meeting

As staffers at *Sassy* magazine in 1989

Partners from

2000 to 2010

Location

New York, New York

Work-wife undertaking

The women's shopping magazine *Lucky*

Pictured: Andrea (left) and Kim

MIKE ROSENTHAL

SHERRY JHAWAR AND ALLISON STATTER

First meeting
Over email when Allison reached out to Sherry about
doing business deals together in 2013

Partners since
2015

Location
Los Angeles, California

Work-wife undertaking
The celebrity and influencer marketing and
branding agency Blended Strategy Group

Pictured: Allison (left) and Sherry

KIM FOX PHOTOGRAPHY

HEATHER COCKS AND JESSICA MORGAN

/

First meeting

On the internet, where they were both writing TV episode recaps,
in 1999; in person in 2001

Partners since

2004

Location

Los Angeles, California

Work-wife undertakings

The celebrity-fashion humor blog Go *Fug Yourself* and
three novels, *Spoiled, Messy,* and *The Royal We*

Pictured: Heather (left) and Jessica

COURTESY OF RADICAL MONARCHS

MARILYN HOLLINQUEST AND ANAYVETTE MARTINEZ

First meeting

In graduate school at San Francisco State in 2006

Partners since

2014

Location

Oakland, California

Work-wife undertaking

The activism-focused youth organization for girls
of color Radical Monarchs

Pictured: Marilyn (left) and Anayvette

DEBORAH JACKSON AND ANDREA TURNER MOFFITT

First meeting

At a women entrepreneurs conference in 2013

Partners since

2015

Location

New York, New York

Work-wife undertaking

The private-funding platform Plum Alley Investments

Pictured: Deborah (left) and Andrea

KELI KNIGHT, YONDI MORRIS-ANDREWS, AND JESSICA REDDICK

/

First meeting

Yondi & Jessica at Spelman College as undergrads in 2002; Yondi & Keli
through a mutual friend in 2007; Keli & Jessica at a Chipotle, where the
three had their first brainstorm about their business in 2011

Partners since

2012

Location

Chicago, Illinois

Work-wife undertaking

The boutique firm KMR Law Group

Pictured from left: Keli, Yondi, and Jessica

PAMELA KOFFLER AND CHRISTINE VACHON

First meeting

While working behind the scenes on the set of the movie *Kids* in 1991

Partners since

1995

Location

New York, New York

Work-wife undertaking

The indie-movie production company Killer Films

Pictured: Christine (left) and Pamela

COURTESY OF HEXIMA LIMITED

MARILYN ANDERSON AND NICOLE VAN DER WEERDEN

/

First meeting

At La Trobe University in Australia when Nicole was
Marilyn's Ph.D. student in 2007

Partners since

2015

Location

Melbourne, Australia

Work-wife undertaking

The biotech company Hexima Limited

Pictured: Nicole (left) and Marilyn

COURTESY OF MISTY MAY-TREANOR

MISTY MAY-TREANOR AND KERRI WALSH JENNINGS

╱

First meeting

As members of competing high school volleyball teams in 1995

Partners from

2001 to 2012

Location

Long Beach, California (Misty), and Manhattan Beach, California (Kerri)

Work-wife undertaking

Olympic-level beach volleyball

Pictured: Kerri (left) and Misty

MATT NAGER

DEB BAKER AND BARBARA DINER

╱

First meeting

On a St. Patrick's Day parade float in 1990

Partners since

2014

Location

Denver, Colorado

Work-wife undertaking

The cannabis packaging company Higher Standard Packaging

Pictured: Deb (left) and Barbara

GALE EPSTEIN AND LIDA ORZECK

/

First meeting

Through a mutual friend in 1966

Partners since

1977

Location

New York, New York

Work-wife undertaking

The lingerie brand Hanky Panky

Pictured from left: Lida, Henree the dog, and Gale

Forging a Partnership

I took your idea, and I made it better.

—LESLIE KNOPE, *PARKS AND RECREATION*

Having a work wife means sharing the burden—and the privilege—of building something, knowing there's someone to turn to who's accountable on both a personal and professional level, and weathering the lows and celebrating the highs as a team (ideally with a balloon drop—which, yes, we've done, though we had to blow up the balloons ourselves). But identifying someone with work-wife potential and then laying the groundwork for that perfect match isn't easy. Even when the pairing comes somewhat naturally via friendship or past work experience, it still takes effort to suss out whether a relationship is partnership material. So what sorts of friendships are up to the task? Are there ways to test the waters before cannonballing in? Given all the risk inherent in a fledgling partnership, how does one go about evaluating whether a pairing will be a good long-term fit?

On Working Together
Before Work-Wifing Together

For us, eliminating some of the fear inherent in making such a big commitment meant looking backward before we looked forward. When we came up with the idea for Of a Kind in 2010, we'd never started a business together (or independently, for that matter), though we *had* worked together in some capacity—and by that, we mean we had taken a college extra-curricular way too seriously. As undergrads at the University of Chicago in the early aughts, we both served on the Major Activities Board. (Note: There was no Minor Activities Board. The name remains a mystery.) We were the group that was responsible for bringing boldface-name musical acts to campus. It's a little curious that we landed there, given that we both call any show without seating a "stand-up concert," uttered with wide-eyed distaste, typically in the context of turning down an invitation from our husbands (e.g., "Yes, I'm free that night, but if it's a stand-up concert, I'm definitely not going."). Our best guess as to why this held any appeal is this: We were power-hungry. We got to run around wearing mic'd headsets! It was intoxicating! So, for a couple of years, about once a quarter, we got a crash course in what it would be like to have a pseudoprofessional relationship with each other and about a dozen of our peers. In between, we'd hold weekly meetings, where Claire would attempt to abstain from over-sharing about her dating life, and Erica would send minutes to a group of people, some of whom thought sullenness was a virtue, signed "xoxo."

A half decade later and eight hundred miles east in NYC, we didn't know so much more about business per se, but we knew a lot more about each other and how we each operated in the world as newly minted grown-ups. In navigating our early twenties together, we'd proven that we were capable of stepping outside our comfort zones and that we could break self-written rules when the situation called for it. It was that comfort level—and a dash of naïveté—that gave us the chutz-pah to start cobbling together the idea for Of a Kind. When we came up with the initial concept, it merged our two—up to that point, totally separate—professional passions into one thing we were vibrating with excitement about. So much of our shared experience as friends was present in the idea: Our appreciation for the fact that if you grew up in small towns like we did, it was hard to uncover the work of small makers; our compulsive desire to discover new things and then promptly learn everything there was to know about them; and our dream of being our own bosses. These were qualities and tendencies that we'd nurtured in each other over the years in the ways that friends do—through late-night conversations, all-day shopping trips, and hundreds of links shared over Gchat.

We sensed there was something about our relationship that could support the weight of a business, but our initial pull toward each other had more to do with the fact that we couldn't conceive of going so deep with someone we *didn't* know as intimately—whose parents we hadn't had dinner with, whose exes we hadn't skewered, whose deftness at leading college students through the paces of large-scale event planning we hadn't witnessed. A comfort level with vulnerability felt like a requirement, and as time went on, the fact that we had played at being professionals together started to feel essential, too. We had a handle on each other's work habits and ethics that made the whole venture feel like jumping into the deep end, but not into potentially shark-infested waters.

Working together before partnering emerged as a theme from the conversations we had with other work wives: Before going whole hog with their online kitchen and home destination, Food52, Amanda Hesser called upon Merrill Stubbs to help research and recipe-test for a cookbook she was writing. Jewelry designers Lizzie and Kathryn Fortunato played at what having a joint business would be like in their late teens, selling statement necklaces to sorority girls out of their college dorm room. Kim France and Andrea Linett started as colleagues at *Sassy* magazine before becoming neighbors, besties, and *then* the creative masterminds behind *Lucky* magazine.

Turns out, the most stable companies are founded by former coworkers, as Harvard Business School professor Noam Wasserman discovered when he studied nearly ten thousand founders of technology and life science startups. Close colleagues share coffee runs and dating stories . . . but also the crushing pressure of deadlines. They have the intimacy of friendship *and* the experience of getting the job done together. Mutual admiration combined with an awareness of professional strengths and weaknesses is crucial when starting a business.

Take Sherry Jhawar and Allison Statter, the founders of the talent and influencer agency Blended Strategy Group, who developed a working relationship over several years before deciding to start a business together. Sherry was the global head of marketing at the beauty startup turned juggernaut EOS (of egg-shaped lip balm fame) and Allison was a talent manager, working with the likes of Christina Aguilera and Jennifer Hudson. They'd done deals together, and they each liked how the other thought. When Allison decided it was time for her to start her own thing—she'd worked for her dad, a music industry veteran, most of her career and was ready to spread her wings—she sensed that Sherry was the partner for her. "We both just gravitated toward each other, really enjoyed working together, and had an immense amount of trust," Allison says.

Allison popped the question while still on maternity leave with her third child . . . and then popped it again when Sherry didn't take the bait the first time. It was on vacation in Thailand that two of Sherry's girlfriends said, "Why wouldn't you explore it at least? Exploring it doesn't mean that you're saying yes." A lightbulb went off for Sherry: "I'm kind of a binary person, and I forget that there's gray." On the plane home, she wrote an email to Allison saying they should dig into the idea. She'd fly from her home in NYC to Allison's in L.A. for a few days so they could flesh out the concept for what would, in 2015, become their agency, which forges direct relationships between celebrities and influencers and brands. Those few days together filled the gaps in knowledge that their shared work history couldn't: They knew they vibed professionally, but, as Sherry says, "it was our personal values—and how close we both are to our parents and our siblings" that sold them on work-wifing together. She continues, "Ultimately, we operate, as humans, in the same way. I realized that's going to be the core of what's going to help us through difficult decisions." It was enough to get Sherry to make the permanent move across the country—where the very first email that Allison ever sent her now hangs framed in her office.

Jessica Morgan and Heather Cocks, the creators of a humor blog about celebrity fashion called *Go Fug Yourself,* are part of this coworkers club, too. They had been friends first, having met on the internet when they were both writing television recaps, and later bonding when Heather moved to L.A. practically friendless. Their professional relationship started when Heather hired Jessica to work with her on a wrestling reality show (that they quite earnestly insisted to us was *actually good*).

During that period, they learned how they each approached work and authority and discovered that they were aligned on

their thinking around both. "Looking back, there was no 'I'm just logging my hours. I'm just showing up, and I'm going to leave as soon as it hits six o'clock,'" Heather explains. "If the cut [of an episode] was in weird shape, Jessica stayed. We both cared about the outcome and about our job even if our job was working on a show about wrestling. Whether we realized we were learning it about each other or not, it was something that was clearly present in both of us. We worked well together." To this, Jessica adds another important shared work value: "We were always on the same page about rule-following. When we decide to veer from the Suzy Rule-Follower, there's a real reason." Knowing from the get-go that they were synced up about what it takes to get a job done right paved the way for them to partner up professionally.

When they started *Go Fug Yourself* in 2004, they approached it as a side hustle—or, really, a side amusement. "It was something to do when we were procrastinating at work," says Heather, playing it cool. But soon they were publishing posts with headlines like "People Who Changed BETWEEN Oscar Parties, Because WHY?" a couple times a day, which Jessica acknowledges was a lot of effort and dedication "for something you don't think anybody is really reading." Building up gradually to the full-time, full-fledged commitment they now have gave them a chance to feel out working together on this project, and it also presented an opportunity to fine-tune their partnership before putting their weight into it. That approach aligned with the by-the-books, get-it-right style they share, something they'd come to appreciate during late nights

spent perfecting reality-TV episodes. And this approach worked: The website developed a cult following and has demonstrated serious staying power, leading to myriad other joint endeavors from reviewing fashion shows for *New York* magazine to coauthoring multiple books, including *The Royal We,* a novel loosely based on Kate Middleton and Prince William's romance.

Even if potential work wives haven't technically been in the trenches together on a job, there are ways to feel out professional compatibility. Shared experience of any sort goes a long way. For Anayvette Martinez and Marilyn Hollinquest, the cofounders of Radical Monarchs, a youth organization in the tradition of the Scouts with activism-focused programming to empower girls of color, that opportunity came annually in the form of planning their joint birthday bash. "Marilyn and I met twelve years ago in graduate school at San Francisco State in Ethnic Studies. We instantly clicked. We're birthday twins," Anayvette explains. "We're both Scorpios: November 16, same year. Only thing that's different is time of birth." When Anayvette got the idea in 2014 to create a Bay Area–based scouting troop inspired by her young daughter Lupita, she knew she wanted a partner, so she immediately reached out to Marilyn, who, she says, "had really similar values and passions around social justice."

Their ability to pull off yearly celebrations—like a Prince-themed party replete with a purple dress code, an all-eighties-and-nineties playlist, and a cake featuring The Artist himself—gave them confidence in their ability to make even

bigger things happen. "I loved the idea of doing it with Lupita, who's my chosen niece," says Marilyn. "I could imagine the field trips and things we could do with her little homies and the badges they could earn. I just got super excited. I was like, 'Girl, this is a great idea. I'm down.'"

"Everything we do is with intention," adds Marilyn. "None of it's thrown together; none of it's slapped together. We had a few experiences planning together, and they always felt very easy. Our flow together is very natural."

Spending time together under potentially stressful circumstances can surface important tells, and there are ways to simulate that experience even for those who don't have a penchant for theme parties. "If [cofounders] haven't known each other five-plus years, I often suggest they take some crazy trip together to make sure they don't hate each other at the end of it," says Hayley Barna, cofounder of the beauty subscription business Birchbox and the first female general partner at the venture firm First Round Capital. In 2015, Barna stepped away from her day-to-day role at the company she'd launched six years prior with her business school best friend, Katia Beauchamp. She now spends her time sussing out the founding teams of startups to see if they have what it takes. That crazy trip she suggests is as good a testing ground as any: The intensity of a cross-country drive or a week in a teeny cabin without wifi allows new partners to gauge how they each act when things go wrong, as things often do when travel is involved. Can they handle each other when a flight has been delayed five times? What about when the suitcase with all the hiking gear never shows up at baggage claim? Far more trying scenarios will pop up over the course of a work-wife relationship, but an adventure like this is a stressor speed round—a quick-and-dirty way to assess whether a pairing has what it takes to level up, and an opportunity to register any warning signs. As Maya Angelou once advised Oprah (yes, seriously): "When people show you who they are, believe them."

On Dating Around

For all this waxing romantic about teaming up with a friend, a former colleague, or, ideally, both, plenty of people are starting from scratch—and in some cases from a place of desperation—when seeking out a partner. Deborah Jackson and Andrea Turner Moffitt, cofounders of Plum Alley Investments, a private investment membership platform, each had trial periods with a handful of other women before ending up together. Who knows if they would have identified each other without having taken the "kiss a lot of frogs" approach.

Prior to working together, they were building separate businesses, and they each tried pairing up with a string of women in their own distinct demographics to do so. Deborah has a prosperous tenure on Wall Street under her belt and two grown daughters, and Andrea, also a former investment banker as well as an author and researcher on women investors, is several decades her junior and a parent of two young children. "I knew I wanted to be an entrepreneur and to run a business, but I wanted a partner to share the ups and downs of creating a sustainable and scalable business," says Andrea. But her early matches couldn't contend with the economic uncertainty and the pressures of juggling startup and family life. For Deborah, the struggle was finding someone willing to put in the work: Her peers were either in retirement mode or couldn't flip the mental switch from the corporate sector to the small-biz one. As she puts it, "The language, the mindset could not get there."

So the two of them just kept swiping right, accepting that not everyone finds their match straightaway. They met each other at a women's startup conference, and, as Andrea remembers, "Deborah and I would get together every quarter and have breakfast or lunch, and I was just watching what she was doing. I think she was watching what I was doing. We kept getting back together." As they continued on separate tracks, their businesses evolved in ways that were inspired, at least in part, by what the other was developing, until eventually pairing up and merging concepts became obvious. Just months after giving birth to her son, Andrea ran into Deborah at another conference. A few months after that, they started exploring what working together would look like and eventually landed on building Plum Alley Investments, which enables individuals and families to invest in promising women entrepreneurs and gender-diverse teams developing new technologies and life-changing innovations. Since late 2015, Plum Alley has closed syndicate investments in twelve companies, deploying more than $10 million, and its members have backed everything from an environmental intelligence technology to an online marketplace for sourcing private investigators.

The way Andrea and Deborah describe it, the trial partnerships and earlier iterations of their businesses now feel like necessary stops on the road that led them to each other. "I think it was, in a way, destiny. At the right time, something appears in your path, and if you're open to it, you will move on it," Deborah says. The fact that Deborah and Andrea are a few decades apart agewise might seem like an unexpected fit, but ultimately their willingness to look outside their peer group for the just-right partner meant landing someone with both shared core values *and* differing perspectives—a dynamic they had each been struggling to find.

But partner dating only gives so much context. In the absence of a shared history, there are other ways to gauge the durability of a partnership in its early days. One cue to consider is how potential work wives interact in front of others. The first thing venture capitalist Hayley Barna examines to evaluate worthiness for her own portfolio of investments is how partners talk together in a meeting. "If they're talking over each other, if they're interrupting each other or contradicting each other, that's a really bad sign," she says. She wants to see pairs who build off each other in conversation and whose skills piggyback off each other's, too. As she explains, "I really like when it's very clear what the superpowers are of each cofounder." In a meeting with a company she might invest in, Barna likes to put founders on the spot and ask tough questions. One she always pulls out? Titles! "Because we invest so early, a lot of cofounders haven't defined titles yet," she says. "I worry that sometimes if they haven't chosen titles that they haven't had a hard conversation." Since there's usually only one CEO, she likes to see whether they squirm when she asks who's taking that role. "If they're wishy-washy or avoid answering the question, it might be a reason for us not to invest, to be honest," Barna adds. "But if they're like, 'We've talked about it. We think it is better for us not to have titles for now, but when it comes down to it, Founder A is CEO, and Founder B is CTO,' that's great." Basically, the fact that they've come to an answer together is more important than the answer itself.

On Similarities and Differences

Togetherness does not equal sameness, though. When pairing up, humans tend to seek out similarity—no huge surprise there. Homophily, the social concept of an individual's preference for said similarity, is well founded in friendships, romantic relationships, and business partnerships. But while sweeping sameness might make for decent bonding, key differences are crucial in professional pairings. "You want to find someone who fills in your gaps and weak points—and vice versa," David Ballard, Psy.D., head of the American Psychological Association's healthy-workplace initiative, told *Forbes*. "This way, when you come together as a whole, it works better than what either of you could do individually."

In preparing for extreme uncertainty, though, commonalities can be comforting, or even galvanizing. In the case of Keli Knight, Yondi Morris-Andrews, and Jessica Reddick, three African American attorneys, a shared experience and value system drew them together to start their Chicago-based firm, Knight, Morris & Reddick (KMR) Law Group. Says Yondi of the catalyzing incident: "There were probably twenty different people in this conference room [at my previous job], and I was one of the only people of color. When we were finished talking about a case, the partner said to everyone—it wasn't specific to me—but he said, 'Okay, slaves, get back to work.' No one seemed impacted by the statement." Stunned by the insensitivity, Yondi took to Twitter to vent her frustration and the intensifying urge she felt to build her own firm. That caught the attention of a friend of a friend, Keli, who responded, "Let's meet to discuss," and motivated Yondi to reach out to one of her best pals, Jessica, to gauge her interest in joining forces.

When they got together IRL (specifically: at a Chipotle), they coalesced around a unified vision for what the firm could be and identified the varied legal proficiencies and disparate personalities they each brought to the table. "The pieces just fit," Jessica recalls. "Our practice areas and what we had done previously complemented one another. Then it just became very exciting." A year later, in 2012, their real-estate-and-corporate-focused law firm was born (and, a year after that, KMR Legal Staffing, their legal staffing agency, followed).

In contrast to KMR's accelerated pace, Christine Vachon

and Pamela Koffler's decision to officially partner on Killer Films was a process, one that unfolded over multiple years and many projects. Yet they, too, cite the importance of this unique balance between shared values and complementary strengths. The two producers worked together on set after set . . . until they couldn't fathom ever working *without* the other. After making the groundbreaking movie *Kids* in 1991, they tackled three more whirlwind projects—*Stonewall*, then *I Shot Andy Warhol*, then *Boys Don't Cry*—which meant seeing each other practically every day. "At some point during that time, I was like, 'This is too good a thing—I can't let Pam get away,'" Christine remembers. In 1995, a half decade into their pseudo-partnership, it was time to put a ring on it: Christine called up Pam, likely on a flip phone, and said, "Why don't we just be partners and produce together?" Pam said, "Great."

"I don't know if it's my temperament or a more female trait, but the calculus of 'I have to understand what's in it for me' wasn't on my mind," Pam recalls. "I was thinking, 'There's something communal about this world I have found,' which is very true about filmmaking. There's something interpersonal that I couldn't even define as being a really big value. When the opportunity to partner presented, it was just a visceral feeling—like, this stacks up in the right way for me as a person."

By then, the two had also figured out that Pam's tendencies to focus on the micro—all of the little things involved in getting a movie from script to screen—meshed with Christine's pull toward the macro—the big-idea, long-term thinking that keeps award-winning projects like *Still Alice* and *Carol* coming in the door—in a way that made them better together. As Pam describes it, "I was very happy for a long time to say, 'Let's make sure the budget gets done,' and Christine was very happy to say, 'Okay, we're good for the next six months, but what about beyond that?'" The success of their union is evident in their impressive track record, with its awards-season nods and critical acclaim. "I guess some people thrive in that one-man-band kind of thing," says Christine, "but if you don't, having that person to turn to who has complementary skills, who is interested in not exactly the same aspect of the many, many things you have to be responsible for, is super comforting."

On Strengths and Weaknesses

Recognizing and reconciling differences and shortcomings in working styles is a fundamental aspect of partnership, and it goes down easier with a sidecar of honesty and candor. For Marilyn Anderson and Nicole van der Weerden, who lead the Australian biotech firm Hexima Limited, which does research and development in plant-derived molecules, homing in on where they each shine—and where they each fall a little flat— has been key to calibrating their dyad (a STEM word for a science duo, if you'll allow it). Marilyn, who was part of the company's 1998 founding team with two other female scientists, set her sights on Nicole as the company's future CEO (a role Marilyn herself never wanted) when Nicole was one of her grad students in 2007, and she recognized in her a shared set of core values. "I knew that Nicole was good because she was doing a Ph.D. while holding down at least one other job, managing a restaurant. I thought anyone who can do this has obviously got good business potential," Marilyn explains. "We spent a lot of time together, but it's like everything: You've got to have mutual respect first. That's absolutely critical." Once they had that foundation, they could get real about the traits they didn't have in common. "You have to know each other's strengths and weaknesses," Marilyn adds. "Nicole has to know that I'm messy and disorganized. I come up with good ideas, but I don't implement them very well. She implements them really well, so it's very complementary."

For work like theirs, it's essential for someone to drive the creative research—determining how to best harness an anti-fungal molecule, say—and someone to navigate more procedural aspects like regulatory compliance, fundraising, and technology acquisition. Rarely is the same person well suited for both undertakings, and acknowledging and accepting shortcomings and blind spots requires vulnerability. Marilyn and Nicole need to be able to present a unified front to their board—with Marilyn as the executive director and chief science officer and Nicole as the CEO—and that requires open-hearted honesty between them. They can't let ego, doubt, or weird power dynamics get in the way. "I'm very careful that I don't interact with the other board members or the chair of the board without going through Nicole. I think that would be wrong," Marilyn notes. "I don't know that this relationship would work so well with two men because the ego is much stronger and they would like to have power." Having achieved this congruence is an especially impressive feat given that they started out with a teacher-student relationship in which Marilyn was an authority figure.

When Anayvette Martinez and Marilyn Hollinquest of Radical Monarchs talk about the ways in which they each fall short—and, let's be honest, drive each other a little nuts sometimes—it comes from a place of real love and understanding. Because they know what motivates their partner's behavior, they're better able to recognize it, point it out, and solve for it. Of the fact that Marilyn sometimes needs to be nagged—"multi-pinged," as these two euphemize it—to respond to an urgent email or to chime in on a pending decision, Anayvette says, "She's a great disconnector." It's a generous read on what is presumably an often frustrating habit—the kind of interpretation that stems from authentic compassion and friendship. "It's not that I'm just, 'Oh, whatever.' I'm so deep in grant mode that I'm like, 'Oh, shit, I've got to come up for air and answer this flood of emails about this, which are really important,'" Marilyn adds. "So I appreciate the multiping and the patience with having to do that with me because, for some, that's not going to work." For her part, she finds herself calling Anayvette out on overcommitting. "I see the intention behind that. She's like, 'I want to do this. I want to be a team player.' Especially in the Bay, there's so much action and marches and community happening. We get invited, all the time, for things. I say, 'Do we really need to do that? That's going to add to your stress level. Let's say no to this because that's saying yes to us.'"

On Gut Feelings

If it's starting to seem like determining the viability of a potential work wife would require filling out some elaborate worksheet, hold on: For us and everyone we talked to, there was an inexplicable *something* that inspired the leap of faith— a belief rooted less in rational thinking than in gut feeling. As Gerd Gigerenzer, a psychologist who focuses on decision-making, once said, "Gut feelings are tools for an uncertain world. They're not caprice. They are based on lots of experience; [they're] an unconscious form of intelligence."

Kim France and Andrea Linett, who created *Lucky* magazine from scratch in 2000 and ran it for a decade with Kim as editor in chief and Andrea as creative director, always had a special spark. Two years after meeting while working at *Sassy* magazine in 1989, they found themselves living in the same New York apartment building, where they quickly realized they shared a worldview and the same touchstone cultural references (that Phoebe Cates issue of *Seventeen*!). They were "like Mary and Rhoda, but both Rhodas." They have a no-other-option, destined-for-partnership tale—and they remember it like it was yesterday, down to their outfits:

> **KIM:** I got this call from Condé Nast, wanting to talk to me about an idea. I went in, and it was to talk about a magazine

about shopping. I was like, "Oh my god, this is the magazine I was meant to edit."

I just knew in my gut there was no way I could do it without Andrea. She had made a fanzine when she was at *Harper's Bazaar* that was full of interviews with real women—everything I wanted to have in the magazine. We were just talking recently about the fact that we both really hate fashion, and we both came from that perspective of a deep suspicion of the fashion world.

ANDREA: Kim called me and said, "I'm working on this thing. Can you leave your job and come? I can't tell you what it is, but I swear you are going to want to do it." I said, "I'm not going to leave if you don't tell me what it is."

You took me to lunch. I remember what I was wearing.

KIM: I remember what you were wearing. White jeans with a big Western belt.

ANDREA: I was such a weirdo at *Harper's Bazaar*—nobody dressed like that. Especially back then, everybody wore Prada.

She told me at lunch it was about shopping, and I was like, "Oh my god. I'm breaking out in hives. When do I leave?"

And there it is—a gut feeling paired with a hive outbreak is an unmistakable sign of *something* crucial, right? When it came down to it, Kim and Andrea ticked all of the boxes for ideal work wives, even if they didn't pay that checklist any mind: They'd worked together successfully before. They saw the world through the same lens but had different areas of expertise. As friends, they were honest with each other about their flaws and hang-ups. Their hearts—and their skin—just recognized all that before their brains did.

Following your gut is the one hard-and-fast rule of forging a work-wife partnership. Beyond that, consider everything we've laid out here more signpost than map, a set of guidelines that we think accurately represents what's made us mesh and, in general, what makes women work so well together. And we like to think we turned out okay.

Learning to Work Together

I want to chime in and be supportive, but I don't know what you're talking about.

—SOOKIE ST. JAMES, *GILMORE GIRLS*

Deciding to work together is one thing. But starting down the road toward actually *doing* so—well, that's something else entirely. To move from talking, brainstorming, and visualizing to opening bank accounts, developing processes, and crossing off to-dos is an early partnership test: Can two people function as a pair not just in theory but in practice? How will a friendship translate to a working relationship, and what is worth letting go of or fighting to hold on to to make that happen?

On Transparency

After coming up with the idea for Of a Kind, we started to pursue it—to quote (somehow) both Ernest Hemingway and John Green—slowly, then all at once. In the winter of 2010, we brainstormed after work and wrote a business plan on weekends. In the spring, we cold-emailed designers and met them for coffee during our lunch breaks. In the summer, we quit our jobs and . . . started to freak out a little.

In August, you could find Claire in child's pose in the shower, bathing in unhealthy amounts of the "What have I just done?" variety of stress, and Erica, rocking in a seat, picturing her office-free, wildly unstructured future. At least those were our states when we weren't contemplating homepage layouts, onboarding designers, developing content, and trying to learn how to charge county-specific sales tax in New York State.

We were feeling unmoored—from the work lives we had known and, to some extent, from each other in these new roles. The person we'd otherwise turn to for comfort was in the exact same position, with all the same questions, uncertainties, and anxieties. Whether we recognized it or not, we were hungry for systems to help us meld our now-very-overlapping worlds. Getting there would require us opening our lives up to each other more than we had as friends.

And so one of our first acts of work-life, work-wife fusion: Sharing our Google calendars. Radical transparency! Not to be hyperbolic, but deciding to make every single thing we do in life visible to each other—from waxing appointments to dinners with former coworkers to meetings with potential investors—feels like it gets to the core of us as a twosome in a meaningful way. It was an act of making things official that didn't involve opening a bank account or signing incorporation documents. In committing to starting our business, we said, "Yes, I fully open up my life to you in the form of a cloud-based calendar service. I allow you to fill my days with appointments because I trust you to make decisions for me and best utilize my time." Our friendship has always been grounded in trust and intimacy, and we have leveraged these same qualities in our business relationship.

There are the obvious logistical reasons for doing this: We can schedule meetings without conferring with each other, a no-brainer efficiency move. We can respond to someone's request for a coffee or a whatever with a "9am works for us!" and pop the thing on the cal. But there's also a second layer of practicality to the method: It gives us insights that in theory might have nothing to do with work but in actuality have everything to do with the states of mind we bring to the office. If Claire has packing scheduled (um, five days before a trip), Erica can wager that she'll likely be a little edgy, because if you're the kind of person who puts packing on your calendar, it clearly requires effort and consideration. If Erica has to brave a morning visit to the DMV, Claire might ready herself for some amount of exasperation, knowing that Erica will have used up all of her (limited) patience by ten in the morning.

Sharing calendars creates a consciousness around what someone's life looks like. Sure, it's the most mundane, color-blocked version of a life, but we'd like to wager that the awareness it gives us makes us more sensitive to each other . . . and maybe even *less* sensitive personally when the woman across the couple's desk oozes irritability. This is a key thing to remember, in any relationship, really, but especially in a work marriage: There are things happening with one of us that have nothing to do with the other, as hard as that may be to believe given the amount of time we spend together.

When you know this level of detail about someone's all day, every day, it quickly becomes natural to send a text to ask how a doctor's appointment went or to dash off an after-hours email to get ahead of what looks like it will be a hectic morning. It sets the stage for openness and constant dialogue more broadly. For the women behind Blended Strategy Group, a full view into what the other is thinking and doing is fundamental to their working relationship. "Nothing really happens in this business without the two of us both being aware of it. We share everything," says Sherry Jhawar. Her partner, Allison Statter, describes their methodology for this as less Google-calendaring-strategic and more all-encompassing: "We're just constantly talking, whether it's email, phone calls, text, or in person. Sherry did not know coming into this that she was getting in bed with a communicator."

On Defining Roles

One of the early realizations we had when starting Of a Kind was how much of our workloads had to do with the minutiae of starting—and running—a business rather than the creative execution of bringing that business to life. And, TBH, the bulk of that work wasn't interesting or exciting. It just had to be done in order to ensure we could process credit cards on the website we were building or to establish a system for organizing product photos.

When there is a lot of crappy stuff to get done, who tackles what? Does it feel fair? What about when it doesn't, which is bound to happen? Perhaps unsurprisingly, gender-based social norms have a lot to do with who picks up the slack and who heads off to happy hour. Katharine O'Brien, Ph.D., now a workforce consultant, did her doctoral dissertation at Rice University on gender differences in accepting or declining workplace tasks. Over a number of studies, she found that women were more likely to say yes than their male counterparts. "Women typically are regarded as nurturers and helpers, so saying no runs against the grain of what might be expected of them," O'Brien explained in 2014. Though this instinct surely has its downsides—it so often leads to being overly accommodating and overcommitted—in a work-wife relationship, saying "Yes!" to any tasks that might come up is both necessary and productive.

This willingness to take on whatever, regardless of skill set, has been a critical component of keeping Call Your Girlfriend's bicoastal podcast operation running smoothly since

2014. Ann Friedman and Aminatou Sow, who forged their friendship at a *Gossip Girl* viewing party, are the hosts, and Gina Delvac handles all things production off-mic. Together they program episodes with current-event catch-up sessions and interviews with guests like Margaret Atwood, Ellen Pao, and Hillary Clinton. CYG isn't the sole income stream for any of the three partners behind it: Gina does other work as a radio and podcast producer, Ann is a freelance writer, and Amina is a tech consultant and media personality. And, as indicated by their tagline—"a podcast for long-distance besties everywhere"—they are not all in the same place: Ann and Gina live in L.A., and Amina is based in NYC. From the beginning, it was obvious which of these three bestiepreneurs— a term that they coined in reference to us but that certainly applies to them—would oversee certain aspects of the podcast, given their know-how: Ann would keep the content calendar for the weekly episodes that tackle everything from pelvic exams to congressional races, Amina would handle biz dev, marketing, and social media, and Gina would spearhead anything related to audio and distribution. But that leaves a lot of assignments that promise to be dirty-diaper levels of fun, and everyone's (extreme) willingness to step forward for those tasks—and to keep an eye on how much time 'n energy is going into such projects—is a point of pride for them. "Like a true marriage of women, somebody always picks up the slack," Amina explains. "I don't think I'm going to ever work with [any other] people who are this competent. I feel like things just happen."

How do they keep tabs when they don't work from the same office or even the same city? Turns out they're pretty good at reading the internet's smoke signals, keeping their eyes peeled for the inbound emails and the Dropbox alerts that mean Amina has locked down a partner for a live event they're hosting or that Gina has finished a cut of the latest ep. In keeping up with the flurry of digital notifications, they're also tracking, in a finger-in-the-air way, how many hours they're each logging in the process. That's something they're especially sensitive to because this is a part-time undertaking for all three of them, and a keen awareness of that is core to their division of labor, as they explain:

> **AMINA:** You know how consultants say, "You only eat what you kill"? We have the mental version of that: If it's your idea or your relationship or you brought it in, generally you take care of it.
>
> There is this flow of generosity also that permeates the whole thing. I feel some weeks I'm just not on top of anything. But I look over, and Ann and Gina are always doing something—so that makes me feel good and very grateful.
>
> **ANN:** There have been various points at which we've all stepped up to do a thing that is really not pleasant in the short term or that sucks up a lot of time in the short term.
>
> **GINA:** We're all conscious of each other's time. We probably move slower than other people, but we understand what the core elements of the show are and everything that we dedicate our time to.

This natural, picking-up-the-pieces approach that Amina, Ann, and Gina have is enviable—but, to be fair, it's not for everyone . . . and by everyone, we mean us. Turns out, we're too type A (or just plain sensitive) for all that. In terms of who takes on what, we need something more structured than the Call Your Girlfriend trio's "eat what you kill" approach, because we're both wary of our toes getting stepped on. For what doesn't fall into obvious buckets—Erica, editorial! Claire, visual!—that's meant divvying things up in a spreadsheet. In the beginning, there were just two columns: the aspect of the business (say, "marketing" or "customer service") and our names (say, "Claire" or "Erica"). You would not believe the sense of relief that washed over us as we fleshed this thing out a couple months into launching Of a Kind. We suddenly felt like we knew what we were doing a tiny bit more—or, at the very least, knew who was going to try to figure what out. It started to give us a sense of ownership—something you'd think would come easy when you own your business but that can be surprisingly hard to come by if a partnership is too fluid.

We revisit this document regularly; it's taken on new columns, new color-coding, and new names in the years since we first created it. Also essential: We make sure the rest of the Of a Kind team has eyes on it, too, especially when we gain or lose employees. Thanks in large part to the dumbfounding amount of clarity achieved by just writing shit down, everyone knows what their job is and knows which one of us to ask when they don't.

For Anayvette Martinez and Marilyn Hollinquest of Radical Monarchs, what started as a loose and casual approach to defining roles has gotten more formal as they've leveled up operations at their nonprofit. Having secured enough funding to allow them both to make the transition to full-time employees, they've been heads-down focused on starting additional scouting troops and growing the number of badass little girls sporting vests with badges in Black Lives Matter, Pachamama Justice, and Radical Coding. Allowing themselves the time and space to see what type of work they each gravitated toward naturally before defining their roles on paper gave them a chance to cater to each of their strengths. Anayvette says, "If there were things more front-facing, Marilyn was like, 'You go do that. I'll handle this paperwork over here.' Marilyn calls herself an introvert with learned extrovert tendencies. She likes to push paperwork, which I hate. Paperwork overwhelms me." As Marilyn puts it, "I love to be that back-of-house girl, making sure everything needed is there so it runs like a well-oiled machine." Anayvette is a self-described extrovert who's drawn to social media, programming, and any aspect of the operation that involves communication and spreading the word. For them, part of making the division fair and square is ensuring that the person who enjoys a task the most—or hates it the least—is the one doing it.

On Splitting the Weight

Even when roles are clearly defined, it's bound to happen that a person will on some days contribute less than her fair share—and on other days deliver far more. The idea that it all comes out in the wash (something Claire says about money but that also really holds for work-wifing) can be hard to process, especially in the early, still-feeling-things-out days of a partnership. That said, it's also an absolutely fundamental notion to buy into: There's gotta be faith that if one partner is ripping her hair out and the other isn't, there will be a time when the inverse will be true. Almost every set of work wives we spoke to had a keen understanding of that dynamic and the importance of honoring it.

For twins Lizzie and Kathryn Fortunato, out-of-step schedules are a given because they're baked right into the fashion calendar that their jewelry and accessories line runs on. The sisters tested the waters of their business idea as undergrads at Duke University, where they funded spring break trips with money earned selling handmade earrings and necklaces to classmates. In 2008, they went official with their label, which has been worn by the likes of Solange Knowles, Jessica Alba, and Helen Mirren. Lizzie oversees the right-brain, creative arm of the business while Kathryn spearheads the left-brain, analytical side. Which means: When Lizzie is designing a new collection, she might be at the office until 4 A.M. on a Friday night. When the collection is complete and Kathryn is meeting with buyers to sell it to stores, she'll work through multiple weekends. As hard as it is to cut bait when the other is in the thick of it—to watch TV, to see a friend, or just to sleep— they're good at protecting each other from burnout. "I'd worked every day straight for two weeks, and on Saturday and Sunday, I had back-to-back market appointments in the office," explains Kathryn of a recent sales cycle. "Lizzie said, 'Do you want me to come bring you lunch?' I was like, 'No, stay in Brooklyn. You just worked your hard month, and now I'm working my hard month.' "

With the blog and book projects that Heather Cocks and Jessica Morgan of *Go Fug Yourself* take on, it's not so clear-cut: They are both contributing the same *type* of work—there's none of this "she's the business mind, I'm the creative mind" or "I'm the tech one, she's the marketing one" element that naturally sorts out who does what and when. They split their editorial responsibilities down the middle, but even though they publish eight blog posts each day, that doesn't mean that they each write four every time. "I think that we both, in our business partnership and friendship, have a sense of fair play," Heather says. "If, day in and day out, she's doing six of those posts and I'm doing two, that blows. That might happen some days. In my head, I'm like, 'I'll get her back another day.' " They also push each other to step away when they can, and they happily—enthusiastically—cover for each other when they do. In fact, during our chat with them, Heather chastised Jessica for not taking enough time off for her last vacation, speaking to one of the most powerful perks of partnership: the opportunity to give both the permission and the encouragement necessary for each other to take a breather.

The reality is, there's no way for everyone to be at the top of her game all the time, and a good partner knows how to provide cover. That's something Misty May-Treanor made clear when we spoke with her and, on a separate occasion, her volleyball partner of a dozen years, Kerri Walsh Jennings. As a twosome, they never once lost an Olympic match, bringing home gold medals in 2004, 2008, *and* 2012 and making the women's game more popular than the men's along the way. Misty, who retired in 2012 to coach (while Kerri continues to play with another partner), cites their willingness to step up for each other as a major factor in their success. "You know people are going to struggle, and it's just keeping them mentally in there. It's accepting that they're going to be off—and knowing what you can do to help. And it's always going to switch—one person's going to be on, one person's going to be off, you know?" explains Misty. The other side of the equation is a partner who's willing to express that they're feeling beaten down, spent, or just plain out of sorts. As Misty explains, it's about "being vulnerable enough to say, 'Help me out,' or 'I just need to put this ball up,' and then the other person accepting them."

On Presenting a United Front

Though dividing and conquering is critical, it's the tasks that get done together and the decisions that get made as a unit that ultimately define a partnership. Even as Of a Kind has grown and we've dished out responsibilities on an ever more granular level, we still put our heads together plenty. For us, a good general rule of thumb is this: If it's a new-to-us project, we typically work on it as a twosome. This means we both know what's involved—how time-intensive it is, what resources are required—and can agree on its priorities. We both contribute to how it should be handled from a creative and executional standpoint. In short: We both have a sense of ownership over it. That shared understanding makes it a lot easier for one of us to take the lead eventually or to delegate while the other one moves into the wings. For example, during our first year, we were both involved in shaping our creative and strategic approach to photo shoots. Even though Erica's entirely removed from them now, she's able to offer Claire informed advice and insights around them, and she's not left questioning whether they're being run efficiently or taking up too many resources. And, perhaps even more importantly, if she ever does question them, she's doing it from a place of experience. This angle on collaboration means that the early days of Of a Kind saw a whole lot of doubling up—and some amount of being too up in each other's faces—but it now allows us to feel we're operating as a "we" even when we're doing things separately.

Barbara Diner and Deb Baker of Higher Standard Packaging are attuned to the importance of keeping their twosome top-of-mind even when they're working independently. In 2014, they both came out of retirement—Deb had been a teacher, and Barbara had worked in marketing—to launch a brilliantly named cannabis packaging company. A lot of their work involves running around Denver separately. One might be delivering childproof plastic jars for housing cannabis gummies to the dispensaries while the other gets the word out about their weed containers made from milk jugs (the first recycled packaging in the legal cannabis industry). "Our clients really know us as a team, so I get nervous when we get so off in our own thing," Barbara notes. "They don't see us as Barbara and Deb anymore then, and I think that's important." As in-sync as they are after nearly thirty years of friendship—they met on a St. Patrick's Day parade float in 1990—it can be easy to lose track of each other for stretches at a time. So they instituted regular touchpoints, like an A.M. call that goes down daily and a shared to-do list (separate from their individual ones) to make sure their prioritization aligns. But even with all these practical tactics, they point to language as the chief indicator that they're operating as a pair. "We always use the pronoun 'we,'" Deb says. That one word tells everyone that they're a team, and, equally powerfully, it acts as a beacon between them, too. "It's a huge pronoun, and it makes a difference to me," Deb adds. "I like when I see Barbara is using 'we,' and I make a really conscientious effort to always use it."

The other linguistic device they—and we!—rely on to convey togetherness, even when apart: Saying "Let me discuss this with my partner." It's a line that's invaluable to any work marriage, providing the option to put off giving an answer, demonstrating a united front, and, most obviously, offering a chance to get the oh so valued input of the other before making a decision. In our case, it's rare that we take phone calls together if we can help it. In addition to hedging against speakerphone fatigue and being just plain efficient, this also forces a nice habit of allowing whatever intel each of us gathers—a new business opportunity or a snafu with a vendor—to sink in before getting recapped during one of our check-ins. Sometimes just letting something sit a couple days—or having to rehash it aloud—can shift perspective. And other times, the one of us who's hearing the news for the first time raises all the right questions about it or is better suited to offer a forest-for-the-trees POV.

On Outside Perspectives

Sometimes, being in a successful partnership requires looking to other people who are less entrenched in the day-to-day for guidance. In the early years of our business, we relied heavily on a handful of advisers—mentor types we had trusting relationships with, who supported us and Of a Kind, and whose commitment to the business we formalized with a little bit of equity. We'd call upon them on an as-needed basis with all sorts of quandaries, like whether what a vendor was charging us seemed appropriate or if they thought spending a week's worth of revenue to attend a major tech conference would pay off. This group of people was absolutely essential then, not just because they helped grow the business but because they also helped quiet insecurities that would reach a fever pitch whenever an unanswered question had ping-ponged between our brains too many times.

Now we have a standing appointment with a management coach to hash out all the big question marks the business regularly raises. Take, for example, the time an employee whose tenure could be measured in months unexpectedly announced his impending departure during a one-on-one with Claire. In response, she pulled a "Give me a minute to think about this and chat it over with Erica." After talking it through just the two of us, we decided this dilemma was ripe for our next sit-down with our coach, a guy (we know, surprised us, too) who we started seeing about five years into the business and whose practical advice and bigger-picture perspective has been invaluable to our partnership. His take: Two weeks' notice was not gonna cut it. Ask for as much time as possible because this person is leaving you high and dry and knows it. And the advice was right. Our employee knew he owed us more than what he was offering and, ultimately, was willing to stay longer if it meant leaving on good terms. Formalizing the process of getting third-party input by working with a management coach (slash therapist, slash marriage counselor) gives us regular access to a welcome outside perspective and also makes sure we're solving hard problems together, as a unit.

At the kitchen and home brand Food52, cofounders Amanda Hesser and Merrill Stubbs find their sit-downs with a professional essential in navigating the transition from their former, sometimes solitary lives as food writers to hectic ones as comanagers of dozens upon dozens of employees. Founded in 2009, their website combines recipes, articles, videos, and retail, and they credit their joint coaching appointments with helping them develop the leadership skills they've used to make their company the thirty-fifth-fastest-growing one in NYC (according to *Crain's* in 2017). When it comes to sitting down with a coach, "Some founders do it separately, but we have found it helpful to just talk through things together," Amanda says. One of the many topics they address during their sessions is the team. "We spend less time on our relationship and much more on learning how to identify the strengths and weaknesses of different team members and how to recognize when people are failing, then how to address it, go through the process of letting them go if necessary, and do that well. One of us might take the lead in the conversation with the employee afterward, but we're on the same page about how it ideally needs to play out and how we're going to support each other to make that happen."

For our part, we do often spend time focused on our relationship in these sessions, but even when we don't, our weekly appointment depressurizes our partnership. Having it on the books means we put a pin in a lot of important decisions we need to make because we know we've carved out time specifically allotted to talking through things. One of the first and most valuable lessons we learned from these sit-downs was that not everything—not even most things—actually needs to get dealt with *right now*, and a partnership benefits from waiting to handle things at a time when everybody's prepared. Knowing we have this sacred hour set aside helps us avoid acting rashly out of an often false sense of urgency.

On Decision-Making

Speaking of decisions, learning how to make them together is a practice that's at the core of any strong partnership. Luckily, being in a partnership at all means making fewer choices on your own, and that also means making better ones. Decision fatigue, lingo introduced by a social psychologist named Roy F. Baumeister, is a real thing—one that leads to worse impulse control, increased procrastination, and, ultimately, lousier decisions. Yes, everyone makes bad decisions, but not having to make as many in the first place leads to improved outcomes. As far as we can tell, though, there's no such thing as "I'm ninety-nine percent sure, but can I just run this by you?" fatigue. Blessedly.

The founders of the prominent lingerie brand Hanky Panky are two women with plenty of joint decision-making practice. They've been working together since launching their business in 1977. Gale Epstein and Lida Orzeck were friends for over a decade before becoming business partners. One year, Gale, a clothing designer, gave Lida a homemade bra and underwear set constructed from repurposed handkerchiefs for her birthday, and it became the catalyst that launched their line. Lida loved the set so much that, with Gale's blessing, she started pitching it to department store buyers. In those days, putting their heads together about their quickly growing company meant meeting up in the New York apartment building where they both lived and where Gale still resides. "Lida was on the fifteenth floor, I'm on the seventh, and neither of our partners wanted us in the apartments to discuss this business. So we would meet in between on the stairs, where we had our stairwell summits," Gale says. Now, getting on the same page involves a walk across the eleventh floor of the two-story office space their $50 million company occupies in Manhattan. "We make most of the decisions together. We don't like surprises," Lida says. "We want to be confident going forward that we are in agreement about everything," Gale adds. Of course, "most" in a company of this size—where Gale heads up design and Lida sales—leaves plenty of minor decisions to be made separately, and for those, according to Lida, "we do let the other one know."

So what about when there *is* disagreement over a judgment one partner makes on her own, or, less clear-cut, with how someone is spending her time? What's the productive way to call that out in a partnership? For Lizzie and Kathryn Fortunato, it can depend on the role. Something they've learned, with Lizzie handling design and creative and Kathryn running the business side of things, is that giving input on a necklace— something Kathryn definitely has opinions about—is different from Lizzie saying her piece about the company's financial procedures for payroll, QuickBooks, taxes, compliance, and all that good stuff that Kathryn manages. "I try to be honest because god forbid I'm not, and then a collection flops because I wasn't honest," Kathryn says. "But on the flip side, I have to trust that Lizzie's done this for ten years really well. The designer knows better." Lizzie chimes in, "It's harder for me to give feedback on Kathryn's role because, what, am I going to say, 'You should file our taxes differently'? I'll make comments like 'I just think it's pointless that you've spun your wheels doing this stupid thing like packing boxes to go to a store when you really should be *finding* the new stores.'"

These two have been at it long enough to know that so many things about their undertaking are unpredictable—which pair of statement earrings in a collection will be a runaway hit, for example—and that giving each other space to do her thing is more meaningful than giving too much feedback. But this only works as well as it does because of their sisterly comfort with directness when they do have something to say. They don't beat around the bush or wait for the perfect moment—they just put it out there. Anyone who's spent any amount of time with them has witnessed, probably with some amusement, their extreme ease with taking opposite sides of an argument. It's enviable! And, frankly, it's something we feel we ought to be better at by now, having worked so closely for nearly a decade. That said: We're not alone in our struggles to get there.

"For girls and women, talk is the glue that holds a relationship together," says Deborah Tannen, a renowned linguist at Georgetown University. Her book *You're the Only One I Can Tell: Inside the Language of Women's Friendships* is a primer on how women and girls talk in their relationships with one another. Tannen observed the dialogues of little kids to root out how female conversations within friendship are different from male conversations. What she discovered is that friendships among girls are largely defined by a sense of connection and joy in similarities, a pattern that continues into adulthood. As Tannen sees it, "if your friend shares your likes, and is just like you, it's a ratification not only of what you like to do but also of who you are." Because of that instinct, pointing out a difference or a differing opinion within a female friendship can feel more personal than it is meant to be. Tannen writes, "Any failure to say 'I'm the same' risks being heard as implying 'I'm better.' . . . And this can be particularly tricky for women friends, given two equally important, but potentially conflicting, values: the special place that expressions of sameness have in their conversations, and the disapproval of any sign that someone thinks she's better." We'll save a deep dive on handling disagreements for a later chapter, but suffice it to say, taking a relationship from friendship to partnership depends on being able to express a diverging viewpoint without the fear of being painted as a know-it-all.

On Listening

Part of communicating effectively is knowing when to say nothing at all. In friendship and in business, one of the most important—and overlooked—skills is keeping your mouth shut but your ears open. Sidle up to our couple's desk, and you'll observe many an instance where one of us is laying down a frustration or a problem, not because we hope the other will solve it but because we need to verbalize, vent, put our ideas in order, and/or just be heard. When that's going down, feedback from the other can be an irritant. Maybe the one of us carrying on knows exactly what she needs to do but isn't ready to deal yet. Maybe she wants to work through it herself in time. Maybe she's just being a grumpy cat. Whatever it is, there's value in another person who knows to listen, lips sealed, when necessary.

Pamela Koffler and Christine Vachon of Killer Films have developed an I-see-dead-people sixth sense for when those moments are transpiring. It starts with their sheer proximity: "We sit across from each other, so we hear each other's conversations all day long, with the idea that every morning we have a download like 'This is what's happening on this movie,'" Christine explains. "Even if Pam's interacting with that particular director, she keeps me apprised so that we can counsel each other." There's listening happening all the time, but that doesn't mean there's a constant feedback loop, even when they're sharing status updates on the projects currently in production. "I know when she is talking to just share info," Pam says. "It's almost like a bird call—like, this bird call is just information, and this bird call is 'I'm hungry.'"

Ultimately, being there for each other in this way—as Pam and Christine are—hinges on being a good listener, which might seem like an obvious skill to apply to a pairing but can be harder to execute when both partners are so close to and invested in the project at hand. Keeping quiet might not come so naturally, and it's something we work on by trying not to focus on what to say next—because preparing a response means only half listening. Instead, we're getting more and more comfortable with the attentive nod, the well-placed "mmhmm," and the sound of our own silence. Often, we've found that staying quiet for a beat instead of jumping right in allows the person talking to go deeper, delving into how this problem is making her feel. (It's also worth noting that Christine and Pam have been at this for over twenty years—so consider their supreme in-tuneness aspirational.)

On Dynamics

Silence can be even harder to come by when there are three in a partnership. Just ask the lawyers behind KMR, who've had to make some adjustments to their interplay in order to ensure everyone's talking and everyone's listening. When they started doing their early, who-does-what role breakdown, it played out like this: Jessica Reddick was the note taker and financial guru, Keli Knight naturally fell into the administrative management role, and Yondi Morris-Andrews was, by virtue of her personality, the talker. From day one, they had a solid sense of how to play to their individual strengths—but guess what? Their strengths have changed as they have rubbed off on one another, gained more experience, and, in Keli and Jessica's cases, started presenting and pitching the business alongside Yondi. Making room for them to do that has made the three of them a stronger unit, but it's something Yondi has to be conscious of pretty much all the time so that they are speaking in a cohesive way and not talking over one another. It is, as they explain, a work in progress:

KELI: When I did get more comfortable, I would want to answer [on a call or during an interview], but Yondi would always answer first. So I think we had to adjust.

JESSICA: We put it on the table, and Yondi was like, "Okay, I'll try to talk less, intentionally."

YONDI: It's funny because even now sometimes when we are on a call or are doing an interview, it's the knee-jerk reaction for me to respond—and it's, I think, the knee-jerk reaction for them that I'm going to respond—so when I don't, there's always a little bit of a pause.

KELI: My phone might be on mute, so I'm like, "Oh! Get off mute."

YONDI: They are completely capable and speak about our firm in a wonderful way, and so it reminds me to try to take a back seat even though it's not necessarily my first move.

KELI: For the most part, I just live not to embarrass them.

Tattoo that last line on our hearts. Committing to each other as business partners who are also friends introduces a whole new level of accountability to everyday actions.

Being in the trenches with other badass, driven women makes you hold yourself not only to your own high standards but also to theirs. Each of us—and our work—benefits daily from the understanding that when one of us does something, we're representing not just ourself but the other, too.

The fact is, for most people, establishing a work-wife dynamic is a pretty new thing. Traditional business environments aren't built to accommodate partnerships, and figuring out how to operate as a duo or trio in a professional setting can take some amount of trial and error and a lot of determination. Among the work wives we spoke with, the common thread that emerged in discussing partnership practices was a commitment to authenticity: Each set of women had determined their own right-for-them rules and routines to achieve professional bliss, but they're all anchored in an honest and empathetic understanding of the personalities at play and the relationship dynamics underpinning them.

The mix of openness, support, and shared grunt work that's required in partnerships like these creates a safe-space environment for professional—and personal—growth. It's an approach that upends so many of the closed-off, competitive, and every-*man*-for-himself beliefs and characteristics that have driven corporate culture for so long—and that's part of what makes it so great.

Finding Work-
Wife Balance

You brought a business card to the sauna? I don't
even want to know where you kept that.

—MAX BLACK, *2 BROKE GIRLS*

There are times—so many of them—when, sitting across from each other at our couple's desk, we start breaking down what we saw on someone's IG story, or this pair of shoes one of us wants to buy, or a disconcerting text we received on our commute in to the office. It's 10:30 A.M., and we haven't quite settled into the workday yet. Or it's fifteen minutes found between meetings, or it's the 4 P.M. slump before the caffeine and trail mix have kicked in. Our employees are within earshot, and they're probably rolling their eyes and/or Slacking each other about us. But you know what? Making room for this sort of sharing is valuable. Oh, hell, we'll go ahead and say *imperative*. We are able to do what we do successfully because we can flow seamlessly from talking about contracts, timelines, and job applicants to Korean sheet masks, health concerns, and C-list celebrities.

While the concept of leaving personal stuff at home might sound appealing in theory, in practice it means not bringing our whole selves to work, and frankly, our work relies on us being 100 percent present—personal drama and all. And let's also be honest about this world we're living in: A clear personal-professional delineation is almost laughably unachievable for anyone in an era when we're Facebook friends with our colleagues and respond to meeting notes from our laptops while watching *Scandal*.

The good news about this decompartmentalization is that research suggests that workplace friendships are indeed good for business—a boon for engagement, productivity, and satisfaction. Per a 2014 survey of 716 random paycheck-earning Americans conducted by the management and employee engagement company Globoforce, 71 percent of the people with friends on the job said they loved the companies they worked for, but only 24 percent of those without in-office pals had the same affection for theirs. And it's not just that people enjoy working with a buddy, either. It's that when they do, their quality of work is better. "Those who [have a best friend at work] are seven times more likely to be engaged in their jobs, are better at engaging customers, produce higher-quality work, have higher well-being, and are less likely to get injured on the job," write the authors of *Wellbeing: The Five Essential Elements,* a *New York Times* bestseller drawn from Gallup studies that span 150 countries. Unsurprisingly, it's women, predominantly, who own this realm: One study found that 63 percent of office friendships are female-female. (Outside the office, men also have fewer close friends than women do.)

A work-wife partnership can lean into the benefits of personal-professional blurring especially hard. Yes, it's handy in an everyday way—because discussing employee reviews while running errands together is just straight-up efficient—but the real win has been not having to bury the baggage of our nonoffice lives. We voice the things that are important to know, as a friend but as a business partner, too—so that when one of us breaks down in tears at the slightest sign of disagreement about marketing strategy, we know it's not actually about marketing strategy. It's about the fact that Erica's dealing with a sick pet bunny or that Claire's suffering from her umpteenth migraine of the month. During the better part of the decade that we've been doing this together, there's been family drama, love life turmoil, and, hardest of all, death, none of which we've had to leave completely outside our 10-to-6. There's been barely concealed crying at the office and pauses in productivity prompted by one of us saying, "Can we take a quick walk?" We've taken turns being the one to say *"Just go!"* when a parent's called in the middle of the day with an important update or if there's been a chance to squeeze in a hospital visit between meetings. On a daily basis, we both make ourselves available, just being there when the other needs to talk—to share a memory or to get upset or to express a wave of feeling that's come on. We allow each other to be real, fully formed, multifaceted humans. That doesn't mean that the balance between the business and the bond always feels right—or that it's something we don't have to work at consciously. But when we put in the work to make our Monday-through-Friday not *just* about work, we find we're more real with each other in our professional relationship, too.

On Friendship

Unlikely as it sounds, being in business with a friend can make it harder to find time for friendship. For better or worse, the periods of personal drama are the moments when it's easiest to make friendship a priority: We can see and feel that the other needs an escape or a shoulder to cry on. It's during the in-between times, when personal lives are taking a back seat to novel-length to-do lists, that it's easy to forget to make time for non-work-related banter and bonding. There's a difference between friends who care about each other deeply and colleagues who just know a lot about each other, and avoiding the latter is a constant work in progress.

The fact that we spend a lot more time working than we do bonding as friends is a being-an-adult reality, but there are phases when the ratio is so off that we feel out of the loop with what's happening in each other's worlds. For every morning spent sharing screenshots we've taken of silliness we've seen on the internet, there are entire days when, despite eight hours of togetherness, we never once remember to ask the other how she's doing. With our work-wifedom well established this many years in, we know that we'll get around to the personal stuff eventually—but that we should probably schedule some time to make sure of it.

Yondi Morris-Andrews and Jessica Reddick know this ebb and flow well. They were close buds before they started the law firm KMR with Keli Knight. In their pre-cofounder friendship, they made a regular habit of shopping and getting meals together, but once they became colleagues, the tone of that routine changed: "We'd go to dinner every Friday, and it became us talking about KMR instead of checking in about personal stuff. I definitely remember feeling like, oh, we're work friends now," Yondi says. "It was easy to get caught up in what was going on with work. Plus, what was going on with work was really exciting for us, and it was what we were so passionate about—so it felt fun to talk about. Then we'd look up like, 'Oh my god, we're done with dinner, and I haven't even asked you about your relationship.' That was a challenge. We had to learn to make sure we were checking in on a personal level. We were such good friends, and it felt like we were seeing each other because we were working in the same space. So you wouldn't necessarily think, 'Oh, we should go shopping.' We'd been together all day." But it was shopping—a hunt for shoes, specifically—that had brought them together as friends in the first place, and they quickly learned that maintaining a friendship within a working relationship means making time for passions shared outside the office, too. Our own personal fix for this has been a habit of gifting birthday and holiday presents that are experiences instead of objects, which sets up the alley-oop for a slam-dunk friend hang at least a few times a year. Turns out it's hard to get carried away with HR chatter while having our ears pierced in tandem, a Broadway show is a terrible place to talk sales projections, and nobody in the sauna wants to hear us complain about cash flow.

These days, Yondi and Jessica are benefiting from the fact that the early-days madness of starting a business has settled down a bit, and they're getting better at making impromptu friend moments happen in the middle of the workday, too. "We had a conference call the other day with a potential client, and I felt kind of funny because my mom just texted me something about my grandmother being very sick," Yondi adds. "When Jessica and I got off, I sent her a screenshot of what my mom was texting me. I remember just having a moment with her over text. It was clear that we started this conversation because of this conference call, but I needed to just check in with my friend at that moment."

At Radical Monarchs, personal check-ins are prioritized as part of the regularly scheduled programming. A few times a week, after Anayvette Martinez drops her kids off at school, she meets Marilyn Hollinquest at Lake Merritt in Oakland for a walk 'n talk. "It takes us forty-seven minutes to walk around the lake. We take that time to check in. 'How was your weekend? How was your day? How are you healthwise? Spiritually, emotionally, financially? How are you as a person?' That leads into a business check-in after we do our personal check-in," Marilyn says. "It's a great energizer, and it's nurturing to our souls and our bodies. It's really important for us to have a work-life balance and to work sustainably. Sustainability is one of our values, and that means physically and emotionally, for us, as well."

That also means that they're keeping tabs on each other's well-being throughout the day. Marilyn might ask Anayvette where things are with programming the graduation for their inaugural scouting troop and in the next breath inquire after Anayvette's stress levels, hydration, and even food consumption: If it's one o'clock and Anayvette hasn't eaten yet, Marilyn will prod her to start warming up her lunch. "We're constantly reminded to take care of ourselves," Marilyn says. "It's definitely a way to keep that balance and embed it in the culture of our organization. A healthy work balance is self-determined. We're doing it."

On Public vs. Private

Ann Friedman and Aminatou Sow of Call Your Girlfriend have their own recurring date—the weekly long-distance BFF phone call that comprises their podcast. Says Amina, "We have different parameters and challenges than other people who are really close friends and even work together since we have this conversation people eavesdrop on." This partnership-on-display scenario that Ann and Amina have may seem specific to the form their business takes, but, really, any work-wife relationship has an outward-facing component. Onlookers—

whether they're colleagues, investors, or just external observers—develop their own read on partnership dynamics through the limited interactions they might have, but the public face a pair puts on is not the same as who they are when it's just them. As Ann explains, "I will say that it is weird that there is a performative version of our friendship—which is not to say it's fake. But then there's a real friendship that we have, and it's a very weird thing to see people outside of our friendship see the performative version and feel like they have some insights." It's not that the way Ann or Amina presents their friendship for all of us to see isn't an authentic representation of it—it's that what gets recorded only scratches the surface of their relationship. It's a taste of their chemistry that interlopers can partake in, and Ann and Amina know well enough not to confuse that with the whole of their friendship.

We have a podcast, too, so we're acutely aware of the duality that Ann and Amina describe. Our first encounter with it, though, came long before we ever entered a sound studio, when we were fundraising for our business. In those investor meetings, we both took on specific roles, and by the time we'd made the rounds to enough conference rooms, we practically had it down to a script. Sure, the people we were pitching were gleaning certain things about our relationship from those interactions, but they were ultimately only getting a glimpse into a small sliver of Claire and Erica—the versions that wore heels, even. (This is how you know it wasn't real.) We've come to value our ability to slip into performance mode when necessary and to slip back out of it just as easily, too. We know there's more to us than what listeners and investors—or employees, clients, and customers—are granted access to.

On Defining Priorities

Drawing the distinction between the work-wife relationship and the actual friendship can be critical to establishing the stakes of a partnership. This was certainly true for Barbara Diner and Deb Baker of Higher Standard Packaging, both of whom came out of retirement to build their cannabis-centric company with a thirty-some-year friendship under their belts. Their prebusiness bond was one of serious closeness, bordering on cohabitation: When Barbara was single, she spent so many movie-and-wine-filled nights crashing in Deb's guest room that it was eventually nicknamed "the Barbie Suite." These two are serious about their work, but they are even more serious about preserving their personal relationship above all else. "I remember one of the first things Deb and I talked about when we started down the path of starting our company was that friendship's most important. Anytime the thing starts to go south, if it starts to affect the friendship, we're done—we're out," Barbara explains of their approach to their venture. "And we've really, really, really agreed to that. We've never had to address it. At the end of the day, there's not enough money, there's not enough anything, to put that in jeopardy." Having established the primacy of their friendship from the get-go has allowed them to set business aims and agendas accordingly. The relationship they've developed over three decades means more to them than seeing their products in every dispensary in Colorado. Sure, ideally they can have both—more, even—but if push comes to shove, the friendship comes first, and the business just goes.

That said, Barbara and Deb's closeness is not everyone's. A work-wife relationship doesn't have to involve best-friendship, and putting on the pressure to be thick as thieves won't do the partnership any favors if that's not what it's built on. For Kerri Walsh Jennings and Misty May-Treanor, for example, being young and green and yet *powerful* made for some quick early-days bonding—they traveled the world together, bopping between volleyball competitions from April to October each year. As Kerri says, "It's kind of a romanticized version of life. You're literally taking train rides from Paris down to Cannes for an exhibition, and you're doing it with your girl." There was wine drinking all across the globe; there was that one time they couldn't get up the nerve to go topless on a beach in France. There were plenty of very hard times, including when Misty's mom passed away during the second year of their partnership. "Going through something like that with someone that you love and care about really expedites a friendship. My heart broke for Misty every single day, and I just wanted to be there for her," Kerri recalls. "Misty never cries—I probably saw her cry maybe five times in our entire career together."

But just because Kerri and Misty were gold-medal-winning work wives until Misty retired in 2012 doesn't mean that they still talk every day or get together for regular reunions. They share a mutual love and respect, but both acknowledge that their relationship isn't one of constant closeness. Says Kerri, "I love her. I miss her. I never see her. But I know if I ever needed Misty, she would be there for me." What they both took away from surviving the ups and downs that come with a relationship like theirs is that a successful partnership doesn't necessarily require putting the friendship first—but it does require learning to appreciate and accept the other for who she is, even if, away from the net, that means getting some distance. That's something that Misty tries to convey to the women she now coaches at the college level: "For, what, twelve years, we were always on the road together traveling, but now people have their own lives, and we understand that. What I try to tell a lot of the kids is you don't have to be the best of friends off the court, but you have to play as a unit." The point of forging a work-wife relationship isn't to transform a friendship into something it isn't or wasn't—to relegate it to a smaller, second-position role or to force it into something all-encompassing. It's to leverage the tenets and qualities of a friendship to elevate the strength of a partnership.

On Other Significant Others

This book isn't advocating for a reimagining of friendships; rather, it's advocating for a reimagining of work—one that, among other things, takes friendships, romantic relationships, family, and everything in between into account. What we see in the type of partnerships we and so many other women have cultivated is an opportunity to welcome and to capitalize on the realities of personal relationships *within* professional relationships. "We really haven't divided our lives into different segments, so our personal life overlaps with our work life," says Kathryn Fortunato, of her day-to-day with her twin-sister-slash-business-partner and their husbands, two men who've had to get comfortable with the fact that they'll likely never live more than five blocks apart. "Everything is amorphous, as opposed to being compartmentalized," Kathryn continues. "That's probably good and bad. It means we don't have any balance—and all the balance at the same time."

There's something unique about the particular strain of nonromantic partnership that we're in with each other—one that's so deeply entwined in love, taxes, and other practical matters that it requires shared bank accounts, a legally binding document, and a couples counselor. It means we get a lot more practice at expressing our feelings and being vulnerable than the majority of people do in their work day to day. As a consequence, work-wifing helps us be better at our most important and complicated relationships in general. As Merrill Stubbs of Food52 says, "I think I've picked up some really important skills from being in partnership for more than a decade—especially when it comes to clear communication and self-advocacy—that have improved other parts of my life." "I feel the exact same way," her cofounder Amanda chimes in. "I feel like I communicate better with [my husband] Tad now." Transferring coping skills we picked up at work to our personal lives in this way can be especially beneficial. We are far less likely to let emotions run the day in an office setting—and all of our relationships could probably use a little bit more of that rationality.

Another unforeseen benefit of work-wifing is that it diffuses some of the pressure that we would likely put on other nearest-and-dearests to absorb the stress of the workday—parents, siblings, other friends, and, most notably, in our cases, our husbands, Thomas (Erica's guy) and Chris (Claire's). In her 2006 book *Mating in Captivity*, the renowned psychotherapist and bestselling author Esther Perel writes of modern-day marriage, "We turn to one person to provide what an entire village once did." (Which, really, applies not just to marriages but to any romantic relationships.) That, she and plenty of other experts argue, is far too great a burden to place on one human. "Marriage was an economic institution in which you were given a partnership for life in terms of children and social status and succession and companionship," Perel adds. "But now we want our partner to still give us all these things, but in addition I want you to be my best friend and my trusted confidant and my passionate lover to boot." It's not that we're immune to these instincts in our own marriages, but we each signed marriage licenses long after we'd scribbled our names on incorporation documents, and we rely heavily on someone outside our marriage—each other—to provide support. We have the strange and truly wonderful experience of navigating, well, emotional polygamy. We each have multiple outlets for our anxieties and enthusiasms, a blessing that, come to think of it, we're not sure Thomas and

Chris fully appreciate—but, oh, would they if we didn't have each other to field some of the bellyaching that happens before we come home for dinner. The privilege of having two emotionally anchoring, centering presences in our lives creates a sense that we'll have a partner to catch us no matter where things land and in turn sets us up to do all kinds of crazy things (like write this very book).

As Allison Statter of Blended Strategy sees it, forging a partnership like the one she has with Sherry Jhawar can fill a void that a relationship or family can't. "I definitely think there was a higher force that brought Sherry and me together. I have an incredible husband. I have three beautiful, healthy children. I'm very, very blessed, and even with all of that, I always did feel like there was just something still missing." We more than relate. The feeling of groundedness that we get from each other is another one of the ways that being in this partnership fuels us: Working together makes life better. Easier. More satisfying. Our friendship drives the business, which supports our bond, which has tentacles that reach out to all of the other aspects of our well-being. And consider the case of the Hanky Panky twosome, Gale Epstein and Lida Orzeck, who recently celebrated their fiftieth friendship anniversary and describe their relationship as enduring, supportive, and inspirational. "We're still together, and I got married and divorced twice," Lida says. (Gale, naturally, made Lida's outfits for both weddings.)

"If given the opportunity to choose our co-workers, why not choose our friends?" asks Courtney E. Martin in her 2016 book *The New Better Off: Reinventing the American Dream.* "We know how to bring out the best in each other. We can more effectively mentor one another through challenges because, unlike a colleague who might be at arm's length, we're aware of one another's history, our idiosyncrasies, and our emotional lives. Best of all: when we kick ass, we get to celebrate together." With this, Martin gets to the very heart of what we're arguing for here: Work can be hard, wonderful, and occasionally awful, but regardless of where it lands on any given day, both the experience and the end result are improved by the knowledge that the people involved are there for each other, not just for the paycheck.

Being Bosses

I don't know who you are or where you came from, but from now on, you'll do as I tell you, okay?

—PRINCESS LEIA, *STAR WARS*

There's a Mindy Kaling quote that speaks to us on an almost spiritual level: "I love women who are bosses and who don't constantly worry about what their employees think of them." Cosign times two. It's not that we're uncomfortable being in charge—we both fall squarely in the category of "control freak," and getting to call the shots on a daily basis is a wonderful way to avoid ever having to address that particular neurosis. But we, like many women, crave a certain level of emotional intimacy, even at the office, and figuring out how to strike the appropriate balance of camaraderie and authority with our team has always been a work in progress.

As soon as we started bringing on employees, the early-days confidence we'd gained in our ability to operate a business as a twosome was upended. It is (we imagine) a similar dynamic to that of coparenting: We had to nurture—and discipline—newcomers together, knowing that the state of our partnership was bound to impact *everything*.

And as we quickly realized, the business-personal divide becomes a whole lot harder to establish when the people steering the ship—the ones setting the tone and the precedent—are pals themselves. It didn't help that our first hires were interns who, sorority life still visible in their rearview mirrors, very much saw us as big-sister types.

It also didn't help that our first headquarters were our apartments. Our dedicated interns would show up early, eager to impress, and one of us, answering the door in a towel straight out of the shower, would have to send them for a walk around the block until their agreed-upon start time so we could wrap up our morning routines. Back at the apt/HQ— everyone fully dressed!—these interns quickly demonstrated how absolutely critical they were to the company's existence: They'd contemplate marketing strategy, build newsletters, assist on photo shoots, write content, track down samples, and function as our fulfillment center, packing boxes, printing labels, and hauling it all to the closest UPS. They would also leave packing tape stuck to the edges of our kitchen tables, stumble in hungover, vodka oozing out of the pores, and find it totally appropriate to break down their dating drama in a group therapy session while sprawled on our living room floors. There was the time one showed up hours late, cardigan buttoned askew, saying she was, of course, sorry, but also had the *best* excuse: She and another intern had spent the night in a threesome with a weird, kind of icky, somewhat famous British comedian! There was the time another insisted upon meeting with us in the middle of Claire's apartment-move day to discuss her internship end date, the explanation for which included a detailed breakdown of all the emotions she was currently processing about her life, her future, her purpose, her values and, somehow, the Vans Warped Tour. (It's hard to believe we RSVP'd yes for this last one, but this is what desperation for help and anxiety build-up will do.)

While a straight-up need for support certainly played a role in our willingness to accommodate these emotional outpourings, so did our socialization as women. From a young age, we're conditioned to be more relationship-oriented than our male peers. As the researchers Amanda J. Rose and Karen D. Rudolph tell it: "Girls tend to care more about dyadic friendships, to more strongly adopt connection-oriented goals in peer contexts, and to feel more empathy for others, whereas boys focus more on agentic goals, including their own dominance in the peer group." Numerous studies suggest that even in a work environment, women have more collegial peer relationships, whereas men have more transactional and informational ones. Mary Clisbee, in her work on education and feminism at Nova Southeastern University, found that though researchers don't agree on *why* there are gender differences in leadership roles, the differences themselves are consistent across various sources and studies. "There was a clear pattern of reporting that women tended to be more collegial and men more hierarchical," she wrote in 2005. "This pattern occurred across research and popular culture material, among quantitative and qualitative studies, and throughout documents regardless of publication date. Embedded in the reporting is the way that power was perceived as either power over (male) versus power with or to (female)." Given all this, it's hardly shocking that the talented, nutty interns in our midst mistook our rah-rah, we're-in-this-together leadership approach for the bonds of friendship.

So does that mean that women, conditioned toward likability and a high EQ, are bad bosses? Heck no. According to 2016 Gallup research, women are better managers who foster more engaged workers—they win at cultivating potential in others and building a team. And when things get stressful, they give *and* receive more emotional social support than men. Not to rub it in, but per this same study, "Female employees who work for a female manager are the most engaged; male employees who report to a male manager are the least engaged."

On Drawing Boundaries

Increased engagement is undeniably an asset, but there's still something to be said for drawing boundaries, especially when it comes to management relationships. By the time we acquired an office that didn't also house either of our beds, we knew one thing for sure: We were too emotionally accessible as bosses, and the work environment we'd created had fueled that. It's not that the early Of a Kind team members didn't respect us or that they didn't get what we were trying to accomplish, it's that we didn't have barriers, which were hard to construct when our inventory was stored alongside our socks.

Here's where we'd love to tell you that we flipped a switch and suddenly became Bosses Who Value and Care About You but Who Are Not Your Therapists, but nah. Our transformation was slow but, blessedly, steady. For all our conviction that we needed to be less deeply bonded with our employees, we still really, really wanted our team to like us—and spent too much time worrying that they didn't or, worse, that they liked one of us more than the other. When we had to dole out critical feedback, we were very emotionally tuned in to how it was being received, always searching for tears welling in eyes.

Turns out spending so much time worrying about whether someone feels that one of you is "the mean one" really starts to cut into productivity. So with each new round of hires we made, we renewed our commitment to drawing boundaries. We started to become the type of bosses who didn't sweat every tough conversation . . . as much. We kept the office environment warm 'n chatty but cut out the no-holds-barred convos. We heard about our employees' birthday plans, but we were no longer invited. We knew significant others' names but not their zodiac signs. The vibe: 100 percent friendly but decidedly not a feelings free-for-all. Which isn't to say we don't lead with empathy and prioritize emotional support when necessary—that's core to who we are, and we think it serves us well. But it does mean that when we encourage someone to take a breather during a stressful time, we don't offer up our living room couches for them to do it on.

Keeping employee relationships out of the friendzone doesn't mean making emotional transparency off-limits, and for Merrill Stubbs and Amanda Hesser of Food52, the latter is so critical to their idea of a properly functioning work environment that they've designed their HQ around it. At their offices in NYC's Flatiron District with light streaming in through giant windows, mismatched chairs invite employees to sit right down and have kick-ass ideas for Thanksgiving-related content. Smells waft from whatever cast-iron chicken or summer-fruit tart is being recipe-tested. The two founders huddle over the corner of a worktable the way they might at a kitchen island—as Merrill puts it, "Our laptops are kissing." All of this creates a decidedly homey vibe, one far better than the actual-home vibes we had in our earliest Of a Kind days. It's also a setup that lends itself well to their notion of workplace openness. Running a business is not all glowing press and rising revenue, and Amanda and Merrill want the highs and lows of growing and leading a company to be visible to their team, too. They intentionally created an office layout that encourages everyone to put themselves out there a little bit, as they explain:

> **AMANDA:** Our friends Brad and Nina, who designed the space, wanted to put curtains over [the conference room glass walls], and we told them we didn't want curtains. Sometimes people are happy at work, and sometimes they're not—and it's okay if people see that. We didn't want it to be a manufactured happy place where you had to hide any emotion that wasn't positive, because that's not realistic. We feel like it doesn't promote a good, healthy culture.
>
> Sometimes when there are really difficult conversations, we choose not to have them in the office. If we think somebody might be sensitive about something, we don't want to put them on display. I think that's the way we design and think about our culture generally: Be considerate of each other and thoughtful about your actions.
>
> **MERRILL:** I actually think it's really important for people to see the two of us having hard moments. The important thing is that we persevere and get through them and that we show that we're working hard to resolve these things.
>
> **AMANDA:** It's not easy all the time.
>
> **MERRILL:** Not showing your humanity . . . I just don't see the benefit in that.
>
> **AMANDA:** There's this fantasy that you're supposed to be the mesmerizing visionary, or you're supposed to be cheerleading everyone all the time. I find that really troubling, and I want to rebel against it.

Merrill and Amanda's efforts to create an environment that is emotionally accessible are a direct reflection of their own interpersonal dynamic. For these two, talking openly about the tough stuff is key to the healthy functioning of their relationship. That they've taken this core tenet of their friendship and applied it to the company as a whole means that the same trust and vulnerability that their own partnership thrives off is something the whole team benefits and learns from.

This by-product of work-wifing—the best parts of female friendship seeping into the way a company is managed and run—is a serious managerial boon. When the PR firm Ketchum surveyed 6,500 people in thirteen countries across five continents about leadership in 2014, they reported a "seismic move away from an outdated, 'macho' model of solitary leadership—a command-and-control approach centered on one-way rhetoric, obsessively controlled messaging and solitary decision-making—and towards a new, more 'feminine' archetype." The traits that polled well among respondents: leading by example, communicating openly, and admitting mistakes, all aligned more closely with women leaders. The takeaway? "The single greatest mistake would be to model the behavioral attributes and communications style of a muscular leadership model that has seen far better days."

On Company Culture

So how does this new model inform a workplace atmosphere? In the case of Food52, Amanda and Merrill's curtain-free office setup and leadership style are more than just management strategies—they're the foundations of their company culture, a concept that is so important but also hard to establish. How much autonomy to give people? How transparent to be? How much to express these things? Is it just an aura that oozes out of the people in charge and the place of business, or is it also a sign hanging in a conference room that clearly states, in a pretty typeface, the company's core values?

Chances are, unless a person has found themself in a unicorn of a role that allows her ample time to just *think* vs. do, do, do, company culture gets established by example, at least at first. The founders of Hanky Panky have had four decades to create the relaxed atmosphere and company pride that radiates from their Manhattan office. There, Gale Epstein sits amid the design team, near the sample makers stitching up lace thongs in rainbow hues, and Lida Orzeck is clustered with the back-office team in a nook decorated with portraits of the two of them and a noteworthy number of photos, comics, and assorted artworks featuring Henree, Lida's standard poodle who recently passed away. (She is still listed on the company website as chair of the board who worked "pro-bone.") According to Gale, Henree didn't come to the office every day, but when she did, she was effective: "If she was in the showroom when we had a customer, she could seal the deal." As they see it, the vibe of the office and the employees who fill it is a direct result of the vibe the two of them put out. "It extends from who we are and the great partnership that we have," Lida explains. "They see fairness. They see common sense and understanding. In all of those things, we try to lead by example."

In our case, company culture has stemmed from the personality traits—and quirks—that we've intentionally or unintentionally woven into the way we run Of a Kind. Claire made a promise to herself when we started the business that she wouldn't let the sure-to-be-insane schedule we'd face get in the way of the morning exercise routine that had become essential to her mental health. Erica, intimately aware of how critical this was to Claire's happiness, was on board to set a later-than-average start time to accommodate it. What began as a practical, somewhat selfish decision came to signify something more: solidifying health and personal time as shared values. Having mornings free means the opportunity for a meal with a significant other (see: Erica's standing Wednesday breakfast date with her husband), a load of laundry, a doctor's visit, a coffee-and-newspaper linger, or a jog around the park.

Because of the sense of mutual obligation we feel, we've learned how and where to incorporate each other's values into our working style, a nod to the fact that when we're representing Of a Kind, we're representing the both of us. So: Erica's insistence on replying to every email that hits her inbox—no matter how unsolicited—because if someone took the time to email, it deserves a response? It's Claire's routine now, too. The elements that anchor our brand—kindness, sense of humor, curiosity, enthusiasm—are the ones that also drive us and our behind-the-scenes relationship. And, yeah: Those are all printed in a fancy font on a sign hanging in our office.

On Hiring

Any effort put forth toward establishing company culture is only realized with the right team. As we've developed a better understanding of what type of environment we want to work in, we've learned what to look for in the employees we're bringing into the mix. Unsurprisingly, we lead with the qualities that have bolstered our friendship and in turn our business. We vet for kindness during the hiring process and zero in on any signs of cattiness. As we've become more comfortable being in charge, we've gotten better at pinning down what *our* vibe is so that we can seek that in others.

This is something that Kim France and Andrea Linett navigated, too, as they established who they were and who they weren't, what *Lucky* magazine was and what *Lucky* magazine wasn't. It definitely wasn't going to be one of those bitchy, stilettos-only fashion offices where people were hired for their pedigree, because that just wasn't in their DNA. The content of the magazine was approachable—more like shopping tips from a best bud than mandates from some high-fashion priestess—and so the editors on the masthead had to be friendly as well. From the beginning, the two of them were aligned on what made someone a good fit as an employee, even if that was hard to articulate to an outsider. "We understood when someone had something to offer, and we understood when they didn't," Andrea explains. "Like, if you believed in an It bag, you were not going to work at *Lucky*," Kim adds. The ultimate compliment from this duo post-job-interview? "Oh, she is one of us." Their ability to tap into that mutual understanding of what made for the right fit helped them grow a team that they felt good about. And it's one of their lasting legacies, to hear them tell it:

> **KIM:** We were lucky for the most part. We made good hires.
>
> **ANDREA:** A lot of people were grateful that they worked there. It was a Condé Nast magazine that wasn't Condé Nast. There was definitely a look on our floor—the jeans dragging on the ground and the asymmetric tops. Everybody knew when you worked at *Lucky*—it was quite obvious.
>
> **KIM:** We wanted people to be happy there.
>
> I do remember [the late *New York Times* media columnist] David Carr once told me that the reputation was that *Lucky* was a nice place to work. I remember being happy to hear that from an outsider who would know.
>
> What I liked is that people formed friendships at *Lucky* that are very important friendships in their lives, and that means a lot to me. To go on Facebook and see . . .
>
> **ANDREA:** Everybody is still friends.

If our partnership has taught us anything, it's the immeasurable value of working with people we actually like. As Courtney E. Martin writes in *The New Better Off*, "If you're going to spend something like eight hours a day interacting with someone, let it be someone you genuinely like, and maybe even love." That's a privilege, and one that we prioritize so aggressively that we've built our approach to job interviews around it. We'll go ahead and call it the fifteen-minute first round, which is a screening strategy we've concocted that is probably very irritating to many candidates we meet with and advised against by plenty of people deemed experts on the topic. It's something we alert candidates to in advance so they don't read into the shortness and so they walk into our office ready to knock our socks off. What on earth can be accomplished in fifteen minutes (aside from an ab workout video and a get-rich-quick pyramid scheme)? Well, we can certainly gauge how a person self-presents—and, more importantly, get a read on their likability factor. Do they come into a room confidently? Enthusiastically? Do they just want to recite their résumé to us, or do they want to tell us why they would legitimately be good for this job? Do they ask thoughtful questions? Do they show up on time? Because the person who shows up late to a fifteen-minute interview . . . well. It's an opportunity for us to sense whether someone's likely to spike the Drive Us Nuts meter before investing any more time/energy/brainpower. And that's really the crux of it: If one of us is not feeling the candidate and is going to throw down a veto anyway, the other doesn't have to blindly spend the next thirty minutes getting to know them. We'd recommend the practice to anyone, but especially to anyone doing the two-on-one dance as we so often do.

Is this a foolproof method? Heck no. But we're not the only work wives with our own, um, special strategy for tag-teaming the hiring process. The Fortunato sisters have their own idiosyncratic method. Says Kathryn: "I do round one with everybody. Then the second interview, I will also do. We make it feel like meeting Lizzie's more of a privilege, so that doesn't happen until round three. There has to be some mystique. If we're both equally accessible, it's kind of bad. We have to keep Lizzie having a little bit of star power. Meanwhile, when someone comes into the office, and they're like, 'Where's Lizzie?' Lizzie's like, 'I don't know. I'm just an intern. I have no idea.'" Lizzie nods along: "That's my go-to response." Hey, whatever works, just as long as the hiring process reflects the primacy of the partnership and the company culture it's created.

On Firing

No matter the kooky, fine-tuned vetting methodology for hiring, mistakes will be made. We've hired a Queen Bee, a Needy Nelly, and someone who made us feel bad about ourselves and our business. When those people were on the payroll, we both felt they were ruling the roost, monopolizing our energy and our headspace. So what happens when work wives make a bad call together? How can they ID it and move forward?

In a partnership, there's always someone to survey—you don't have to rely on one read alone. Which is a win in hiring, for sure, but also in knowing when someone's gotta go.

Amanda and Merrill of Food52 have some thoughts on this topic. Their (horror) story about bringing on an employee who ended up poisoning the water illustrates the ways in which navigating these HR challenges together delivers real benefits. In being able to turn to each other and to make this call more quickly than either would've on her own, they were able to be better, more efficient managers to the Food52 team members—all of whom, they soon realized, were just as affected by the booted employee's toxicity as they were. It taught them, as they explain, how firing could make the team stronger:

> **AMANDA:** We got bullied by someone we hired, and it was terrible. It was a long period of intense, silent bullying. That was a really tough professional experience, getting through that together—and also getting to the point where we recognized, "Wait a second, we're being bullied. This is wrong. Why are we letting this happen, and how are we going to fix it?"
>
> When you get bullied repeatedly, you lose your confidence. We had lost a lot of confidence about our ability to lead, and that makes it especially hard to let someone go. Once we realized this was what was going on, it was like, "We're grown-ups. We can figure this out." I actually do think that was a big turning point for us, letting that person go.
>
> **MERRILL:** We weren't the only ones on the team who felt relief, and that was very clear.
>
> With hiring, it's a constant process of improving your radar because I do think that some people are good at

hiding it. But there are indicators that you can pay attention to. I think we've gotten better at recognizing them. There are still times when we miss them.

AMANDA: I think we generally want to give people a chance—we tend to be more optimists than skeptics about hires.

Accepting that firing is always going to be part of the job description as bosses is a solid lesson to take away from these two. And that means getting good at letting people go, or at least comfortable with it. Of course, this never comes easy, even when it's clearly the right thing to do—and especially if, as a twosome, it can feel like ganging up on someone. Often it takes one of us, usually the one of us with a little more distance from the situation, to say to the other, "Okay, I've heard you complain about this for long enough, and I think so-and-so might not be working out."

For us, the best approach has been to make the process as shock-free as possible. We're committed to communicating expectations and shortcomings to the underperforming employee clearly—so there's a natural escalation that happens. We have one-on-one meetings with lines like "Hey, you really dropped the ball on this. What can I do to help make sure that doesn't happen next time?" If those meetings don't make any headway, we move into regular check-ins with both of us. During those sit-downs, the goal is still getting us all out of this rut, but if there isn't progress—and there should be clear goals on what progress would look like!—then we head into a final chat that kicks off like this: "This shouldn't come as a surprise based on the conversations we've been having." Typically, Erica delivers the tough-to-swallow news and anything logistical that needs to be communicated, and Claire expresses both gratitude and empathy. The point is not to make this feel formulaic or robotic but to give each of us only so much to focus on, because it's tremendously stressful and emotionally draining to impact people's livelihoods in this way. We want to do as right by anyone who's worked for Of a Kind as we can, and, as with most business-related things the two of us do, that means splitting up our roles effectively.

On Comanaging

A strong bond between the individuals leading a business can set a great example for employees, but it can also feel like a great big barrier to entry. Amid all the pros of our friendship sitting at the heart of the biz we've built, there are cons, too. Even as we've found those people who mesh with our mission statement and better the business, they aren't the two of us. That has been a shockingly hard lesson for us to learn: Each of *us* can intuit what the other one is thinking with relative accuracy, but that makes it all too easy to forget that it is absolutely insane to expect that of anyone else. This hang-up rang especially true for Lizzie and Kathryn Fortunato in the beginning of their partnership—what with their twin mindmeld and all. Says Kathryn: "I found that we got frustrated with our team a lot more easily—because Lizzie and I would think about something the exact same way, but why would they think about it that way?" Lizzie adds, "It was so much easier being frustrated instead of just being like, 'Okay, I'm gonna teach them this so they know.' They had to get our way of life—we knew we had the same standards about everything."

Sherry Jhawar and Allison Statter of Blended Strategy Group have made conveying their closeness a critical part of their leadership strategy. "One of the things that Sherry and I talk a lot about is making sure that the team knows how much Sherry and I communicate," Allison explains. "If Sherry's working with someone on something directly or I'm working on something directly, it doesn't mean that the other is out of the loop on it. It just means that that's what the line of communication is." To make this known, Allison will go out of her way to give props on specific achievements to someone who works primarily with Sherry (who will do the same with Allison's reports), demonstrating that whether or not both partners are directly involved with managing a person or a project, they are each keenly aware of how it's going. "It's really important that they know that we both know how hard they're working and what they're doing," Sherry says. Same goes for when an employee is falling short and it's time for tougher feedback of the sort that might surface during formal reviews. "Though we divide-and-conquer filling out the review questionnaires, Sherry edits mine and vice versa, and we sit and do the reviews together to make sure that the feedback they are given is joint feedback," Allison notes. Their commitment to this approach extends even to the moments when the two of them aren't syncing up so seamlessly. "We disagree and sometimes fight in front of our employees," says Sherry. "I'm a big believer in 'If the kids don't see you fight, then when they do, they think you're breaking up, and they freak out.' The team has seen us fight, and they know that we're still Bert and Ernie."

Still, putting all that closeness on display can come with a risk of leaving others feeling that they're always on the outside. It's something the two of us grapple with regularly: We never want to project a vibe that we are part of a club that's closed for membership. But according to psychologist and (our!) management coach Dr. Ben Michaelis, some amount of this is fine—and even necessary. "You don't want to come off as cliquey, but it's okay for cofounders to be able to connect to one another in a way that their employees can't one hundred percent access," he says. "I'd be more concerned if your relationship to an employee looked exactly like the relationship you have with your cofounder."

Marilyn Anderson and Nicole van der Weerden of the biotechnology firm Hexima didn't just fear their employees being intimidated by their closeness—they witnessed it firsthand. It was a nearly inevitable consequence of Marilyn plucking and grooming Nicole for the CEO role. Marilyn had been part of the 1998 founding team at Hexima, and when Nicole joined in 2007, there were scientists and researchers on the team—some of them with more tenure—who didn't understand why *she* was so special and didn't know what to make of her bond with Marilyn. "Immediately, we had to learn to move those people on. We got other jobs for them," Marilyn says. "The facts were that Nicole was in that role, she'd been selected, she was performing, and they weren't going to be given that role. And there was no room for jealousy." Talk about a take-no-prisoners-or-bullshit referendum: It became perfectly clear that collegiality was a job requirement.

These days, the bond that Marilyn and Nicole share is simply part of the company's fabric. And just as their team accepts the nature of their work-wife relationship, the two of them recognize the different, and sometimes codependent, leadership roles they each take on in managing their staff. "People know to come and talk to me if they want to tell Marilyn something that they're not game enough to come and talk to her about," Nicole says, acknowledging that some on the team are too in awe of Marilyn to take things to her directly. "Even though Nicole's the boss, she's also a peer," Marilyn explains. "She's part of the Hexima indoor soccer team that plays socially in a local competition. They're friends, and that's why they often will talk to Nicole about things they would with their other friends."

Having two very different personalities like Nicole and Marilyn at the helm of a company means the potential for complementary management approaches and richer relationships to leadership. But . . . does it end up driving people insane? Isn't it hard enough to figure out one kookalook boss with her weird dietary preferences and Monday-morning meeting intensity? Not if partners know how to work it and are comfortable with the different roles they play. This requires a spot-on understanding of what each brings to the table—a self-awareness that Christine Vachon and Pamela Koffler of Killer Films both possess. They've taken it upon themselves to help employees navigate the nuances and particularities of working with the other. Since Pam knows Christine's idiosyncrasies—and might even be able to verbalize them better than Christine could herself—she's well equipped to pass along the intel necessary for someone to get it right with Christine. They do things differently, and they're great at recognizing, appreciating, and catering to that fact:

> **PAM:** Sometimes an employee comes to me and says, "I feel like I'm messing this thing up with Christine all the time. What am I doing wrong?" I say, "Okay. Let's analyze it." It's usually about Christine's travel. "Are you thinking this through? Even if she says this, you know she wants that." It's a little like being two parents sometimes.
>
> **CHRISTINE:** We have very different styles in the way we work. There are people that are better suited to Pam's style and people that are better suited to mine.
>
> I think I've changed a lot. I think Pam used to have to clean up after me a little bit more because I blew up at somebody—you know, that kind of thing.

Listen, being cobosses can be weird. It certainly gets easier after doing it for as long as Christine and Pam have, but at the end of the day, there's not just one right way to do it. What's made it work for us is figuring out *our* way, which we could only do once we'd defined exactly what was important to us. Number one on that list is our partnership and structuring things in a way that protects it. Number two is the people who work with us—making sure they feel respected, heard, and supported. Number three? Making room for us each to express our own individual versions of crazy and, heck, even baking those quirks into the way the whole team operates. Talk about a perk of being in charge.

Dealing
with Money

I'm not sexually aroused; I'm fiscally aroused.
—ILANA WEXLER, *BROAD CITY*

H ere's something you didn't need to buy this book to learn: Centuries of oppression have left their mark on women's relationships with money. Statistically speaking, we are less comfortable talking about it, feel self-conscious (or worse) if we make too much of it, and face all sorts of hurdles on the path to getting it. A study by Fidelity Investments found that of 1,542 women surveyed, 80 percent avoid financial convos because they're "uncomfortable" or "too personal." We're more likely to talk about health issues and sex than salary and investment ideas. And that earning-too-much thing? The University of Chicago Booth School of Business conducted a study of four thousand married heterosexual couples in 2013 and found that once a woman started to make more than her husband—even if only by a margin as small as $5,000—their chances of divorce increased. And! Regarding those hurdles, here's just one of them: In 2016, companies run by men got sixteen times the VC funding of companies run by women.

If financial stuff comes with all sorts of baggage for one woman, you can bet it gets more complicated when multiple women are involved. When it comes to work-wifing, money is the perpetual third wheel. There's one partner, there's the other partner, and there's the money the business is making or not making, spending or not spending. There's also the need to get aligned on a lot of complicated issues: the ideal scale of the enterprise, how much money to raise and spend to get it there, and what each partner needs to be taking home in order to make the pursuit not just worthwhile, but also feasible. They're topics that can feel daunting to tackle mentally—and even more so to talk about frankly—but approaching them with openness, empathy, and candor makes shambling through them infinitely more viable.

On a Common Approach

Though diverging mindsets can be a boon for some aspects of work-wifing, it feels safe to assume that there are few, if any, business partnerships that have found success without first finding a shared POV on the topic of finances. For all the money issues we each brought to the table when starting Of a Kind, the one anxiety we did *not* have was whether the other would mishandle it. That we meshed as well as we did in this realm—and continue to do so—was not a given. Our money management styles have very little in common when it comes to our own personal finances. We each have a whole host of inexplicable quirks (there are sticky notes involved) and complicated psychologies to back it all up. But for a number of reasons—those shared values we talked about earlier, combined with a healthy amount of fear and a similar position in life—our mentalities synced right up around business balance sheets.

We saw Of a Kind as an opportunity to pursue an idea that we found wildly exciting and hopefully to make careers from that. The focus of our early days wasn't on getting rich quick or really even getting rich at all. Our aim—something we discussed at length—was to conserve enough money so we could keep this thing running long enough to make a real go of it. We were both young (twenty-six and twenty-seven) and in possession of varying degrees of uncertainty and doubt about the vocations we'd chosen out of college. Neither of us sacrificed a huge salary when we quit our jobs, neither of us had a family to support, and neither of us was counting on retiring in our thirties. All of these factors helped us align on how much money we were expecting to make from these new jobs we'd created, how soon, and the budgeting that would get us there. To summarize our early-days approach to finances: We were very scrappy—and proud of it.

Similarly for Christine Vachon and Pamela Koffler of Killer Films, being aligned not only on their approach to money but also on how much money *matters* is core to their success as partners. They make movies, but not the kind earning summer-blockbuster, superhero-franchise returns. Instead, they've taken the indie route and have opted to prioritize telling the sorts of stories—about women, about gay people—that often get less big-screen time. "We have been good partners, in part, because the hierarchies of our personal values are pretty in line. Money is not the absolute top priority," Pam says. "There were many, many times when Christine would say, 'I really think this is what we need to do with this money,' and it wasn't in either of our best interests." Knowing what they, as a team, value simplifies conversations and decisions around monetary stuff. If making a film with an important story that might not otherwise see the light of day takes precedence over making bank, choices suddenly become simpler. *"Beatriz at Dinner* is a good example, because on paper that movie didn't make any sense," says Christine of the 2017 film they produced starring Salma Hayek about inequality, immigration, gender, and power. "We were earning, like, less than chump change. It cost us money. But we both felt very strongly—if we were going to do one of these projects this year, that was the one."

The Killer fiscal mindset doesn't align with the spendy, swing-for-the-fences, go-huge-or-go-home attitude heralded by today's business culture, but these two make sticking to one's guns look both aspirational and downright essential. As Pam explains, "I do think one of the reasons we have managed through the feast-or-famine nature [of filmmaking] is we've never been profligate. We never got to that place where we had a fancy office and a lot of staff because then it would have all come crashing down." When the two of us sat down with Christine and Pam around a large, shiny conference room table, they wanted to make sure we knew it was not *their* conference room table—they split an office with another company and seemed to take a lot of pride in the thriftiness that signaled. It was encouraging to breathe in the secondhand confidence wafting off two women who had zero qualms about the fact that, twenty-odd years into it, their business is still lean and their meeting space still shared. Killer is small—but mighty enough to have won two Academy Awards and to have been nominated for eleven more.

This you-don't-have-to-be-gigantic-to-be-great mindset is one we're comfortable with now, but when we were starting out, it felt like an admission of limited vision or ambition. There was pressure to raise mountains of money from venture capitalists—something the media amplifies by writing about a company's $10 million in funding as if that in itself is proof of success. Companies that don't plot a path involving eight-figure rounds of investment are likely to be labeled "lifestyle businesses," a decidedly pejorative term within the startup community we were surrounded by during our early years. What's a "lifestyle business"? It's one that's intended to sustain the lifestyle (i.e., income) of the people who own it. It's not a company being built for a billion-dollar acquisition or a future listing on the NYSE. Which isn't to say it can't or won't make a lot of money—just that if it does, it's the founders who are going to get rich instead of investors or shareholders. As a term, it doesn't have to be a diss, but it's often used as one—and, it comes with a dose of implied gender discrimination, too. According to the 2013 Women-Owned Business Report from American Express OPEN, the annual revenue of women-owned businesses nationwide hovers right around $155,000, as compared to the national average of $400,000. (Keep in mind that revenue is not the same as profit, so bigger does not necessarily mean better.) More women, on average, are creating lifestyle businesses, and using that term as a put-down is meant to make them and what they're architecting feel small in an ecosystem that privileges a historically male, high-risk approach.

Though this dynamic is clear to us now, it wasn't when we started out (or for many years after that), and our own lack of clarity around how big Of a Kind could or should be and how it would get there meant a lot of wasted time succumbing to the pressures of what we assumed Silicon Valley investors or *Forbes* magazine editors were interested in seeing. While we ultimately set our sights on Of a Kind being more mighty than huge, there is obviously absolutely nothing wrong with plotting an IPO from day one. (Please! Do it! And once you tire of swimming, Scrooge McDuck–style, in your hard-earned piles of gold coins, go invest in some other women-led businesses, will you?) As Deborah Jackson, one of the former Wall Streeters behind the female-centric investment platform Plum Alley, put it to us, "There's nothing wrong with making a lot of money. That's the thing—it probably means you have a great business. You can care about something, but it can also be a business. They're not mutually exclusive."

For Gina Delvac, Aminatou Sow, and Ann Friedman, the trio behind Call Your Girlfriend, those two concepts *were* effectively exclusive in the beginning ("the early hobby days," as Gina describes them), before their pop-culture-and-politics podcast started to look anything like the business it is today: one replete with a listenership in the hundreds of thousands, regularly sold-out live shows, and always-in-demand merch. Twelve months after they first started recording their weekly long-distance bestie conversations and putting them out into the universe, their first ad sale to Squarespace finally gave them cause to open a bank account together. It's the moment they identify as CYG's official metamorphosis from a friend collab to what they now jokingly refer to as a "micro-business," and that transition led to emotional and psychological shifts for all three of them. As Gina recalls, "It was like we understood that once we were selling ads, we also should be more consistent with our product. It was this process of trying to level up to have the capital we needed to support the time we were spending." Adds Amina, "I had intellectualized that it was going to be a business—we had an LLC—but, for me, that was like, 'Oh. We're doing this for real.'" For them, "doing it for real" has meant more than just making money and being accountable to advertisers. It's also meant aligning on financial philosophies to ensure they reflect the same personal and professional politics they espouse on the show:

AMINA: It's very important to me that everybody is compensated for their time. It feels really fucking awesome when
we can cut bonuses to our support people and we can pay
people to make us Instagram filters or to make us new
music or to be able to afford the things we really want. It's
important to me as a feminist. It's important to me as
someone who cares about money and generating wealth.
We worked really hard on this thing, and knowing that it is
profitable and that there is a model for it—you can learn our
politics and see them in play.

ANN: Money's important to me, not in a sense of "I need to get
rich as a result of this podcast," but definitely in the "I want
us to be compensated for the time that we put into it." And
I agree that it feels really good. Our friend who composed a
bunch of custom music for us would have done it for free.
But we could be like, "You're a professional who does this for
a living. We want to pay you a market rate to provide a
service for us." We could not do that if we were a not-for-
profit that never took any advertising, so that feels really
good.

Money also creates real stakes and real rewards for us.
We were always, from the beginning, committed to each
other—and we were still showing up to do this consistently
before we made a penny, which was a long time—but there
is something about being like, "We're not just three-way
partners in a side project. We're making money. We're
accountable to people." That feels like it's made the product
better because we're more serious about it.

For CYG, being able to manage the monetary aspects of their business in a way that reflects their beliefs is fundamental to their operation. Whatever that looks like for another work-wife duo, trio, or quartet, the thing that's non-negotiable is that everyone is in agreement on what the big plan is.

Finding that alignment requires constant discussion about money and expectations related to it, no matter how unnaturally that may come, and no matter how often those expectations may shift. The place a partnership starts on this front may not be where it ends up. Nine years of ass-busting behind us and dreams of paid-off credit cards, home mortgages, and swelling savings accounts ahead of us, making money has started to feel a lot more important, and the aims of our business have shifted accordingly. Where being scrappy was once the core virtue we led with, now we think more about payoff, ROI, and compensation. We want to make a lot of money, and we're not here to be judged for it. That we're on the same page about this outlook now—and through its various evolutions over the years—has always been a critical aspect of our ability to partner effectively.

On Funding and Equity

The importance of shared financial expectations in a successful business partnership cannot be overstated. From there, the next steps are figuring out what each partner is putting into it and getting out of it—and where else to go digging for money beyond personal bank accounts.

There are about as many ways to go about funding a pursuit as there are Kardashians, and they all take ample effort, energy, and sometimes dumb luck. There are small-business loans, which are hard to come by in today's banking climate; grants, which can seem like a fingers-crossed crapshoot; angel investors, the rounding up of which can feel like herding (rare breed) kittens; venture capitalists, who are looking for eye-popping returns and an equally showy pitch. And those are just the most obvious ones.

Shoring up capital is pretty miserable—we're not going to lie—and so many great business ideas never get off the ground because of lack of access to capital, an issue that's only compounded by racism, sexism, classism—basically all the isms. (If you've ever wondered about the lack of innovation in breast pumps, male birth control, or treatment for lupus, a disease that disproportionately impacts black women . . . there's your answer.) A study by the VC firm First Round Capital found that though founding teams that include women outperform all-male-led teams by a whopping 63 percent, female CEOs get a meager 2.7 percent of all venture funding. For women of color, the statistic is even worse; a mere 0.2 percent of funding goes their way. Having even one woman on a team dramatically *decreases* a company's likelihood of raising capital compared to an all-male team. And it's not just women in the startup world getting squeezed: Another study found that women have a harder time getting bank loans for their businesses than men. Most end up using personal savings to fund their companies, which means they're generally starting out with less capital and may have to shrink their goals accordingly. Despite all these financial barriers, women start twice as many businesses as men—a middle finger to this particular manifestation of misogyny.

In the case of Of a Kind, we were very, very fortunate to have access to capital from loved ones, since without it, as the numbers suggest, our business might never have happened. We got off the ground with a $200,000 investment and raised an additional $300,000-ish from friends, family, and one professional investor over the next five years. We recognized then, and now, that this was an *extremely* privileged place for us to be starting from. We also recognized that it was a limited funding source and that prospects for additional capital raises in the future were uncertain, so our practice from day one was to spend as little as possible. The ethos, especially of the first few years, boiled down to the following: If we could avoid paying for anything, we would. As in, we once traded web development hours for style consulting, Claire's grandma's house was Of a Kind HQ West for our quarterly business trips to L.A., and we somehow convinced an overeager nightclub manager to hold a glitzy launch party with hundreds of guests for a cool thousand bucks. We weren't afraid to ask for help or favors, and we held ourselves to the same high operational and customer service standards set by our VC-backed peers.

Once we'd opened our first business checking account— and had photos taken with the banker who facilitated it, naturally—we got down to the brass tacks of ownership. Enter: the equity conversation, a talk that led to our first major work-wife disagreement. We had some of our first really hard discussions as nascent business partners on this topic—there were conference calls with the two of us and lawyers. All the anxieties, insecurities, and potential resentments we were both feeling surfaced as argument points: Who had quit her job first, who was giving up a bigger salary, who had brought more investment dollars to the table, who was more committed to this thing from the get-go, who had already made a bigger contribution up to this point, and who would make a bigger contribution overall? These conversations truly sucked and at the time felt like the first big beast we'd have to slay in order to prove to ourselves—and everyone else—that we were up for the larger challenge of starting this business together.

Here's the thing about that whole equity conversation: We never really found common ground, but we did ultimately privilege the funding that allowed us to get off the ground in the first place. When we signed the incorporation papers, Claire owned 50 percent of the company, Erica owned 30 percent, and the remaining 20 percent was put in a pool set aside for advisers, investors, and employees. Conversations about money and ownership at such an early stage of a business are predicated upon about a million and one unknowns, and at some point we just had to decide to move on. Unless the business finds some amount of success, it's all moot: 50 percent of zero is the same as 30 percent of zero. That said, it was a tough thing to settle into, to get comfortable with. It's hard to know what to value in what order—experience, connections, cold hard cash?—because all of those things matter more or less from business to business. There's no good rule of thumb except not to let it be the thing that tears a partnership apart.

This is a concept that becomes even more complex—and, arguably, even more important—if business partners are related. "I remember my mom saying, 'You can't have a business that gets between the two of you,'" Kathryn Fortunato recounts of the early days of the jewelry business she started with her twin, Lizzie. So they formalized exactly what their operating and ownership structure would look like: "We really went deep: If we have a financial disagreement, I get final say. If we have a design disagreement, Lizzie gets final say," Kathryn adds. "If we can't work it out, we'll name three mediators to mediate a disagreement. We hired a lawyer who, early on, my mom set us up with. She was like, 'Put this in writing.'" And though it might seem like their equity split (fifty-fifty from the beginning) should have been an easier road to navigate given their twindom, it wasn't necessarily that simple: These two are a textbook case of sweat equity vs. cash investment. When they were starting out, Lizzie was working on their jewelry label full time while Kathryn held down an investment banking job. That Goldman Sachs gig of Kathryn's is what allowed Lizzie to jump in with both feet: On their twenty-third birthday, in 2007, Kathryn wrote a check for $10,000 and left it on their kitchen table for Lizzie to find. "That was the money we started the business with—that one check," Lizzie says. "I had, like, zero dollars in my bank account at the time. We would sell a necklace on consignment, and the store would call and say, 'Come pick up a check—you have a hundred and sixty dollars here.' That was my income." When cash flow got tight, Kathryn would lend additional financial support to tide the business over. Though she felt lucky to be in a position to do that, it wasn't emotionally easy on either of them, and they both have the angsty memories to prove it:

> **KATHRYN:** I do remember having a few nights of resentment where I was like, "I'm subsidizing Lizzie, to some extent."
>
> I remember getting home one night, and Lizzie had left to go out without me. I remember crying to Kate [our roommate] that all Lizzie cared about was being a cool little baller, and I was working all these hours to make the money and pay the electric bills.
>
> **LIZZIE:** I remember that, too, vaguely. I probably felt guilty and sad, but then I also remember me always saying, "What you're putting in in equity, I'm putting in in sweat equity." We would fight about that because I would always have to stay up really late to make jewelry. I don't know why I was so busy, but it would be four A.M., and I was finishing a necklace.
>
> My argument was always, "I'm working Goldman Sachs hours, and I have zero money. You're working Goldman Sachs hours, and you have a lot of money."
>
> **KATHRYN:** And zero fun—because you did have a lot of fun.

In 2010, Kathryn left her job to join the accessories business full time after what they describe as an Oscar-worthy "life's too short" speech from Lizzie that included the line "No one's gonna do this for you. You don't have to do it, but stop saying you're gonna quit your job. Just quit your job." At that point, the time vs. money argument became irrelevant— they were both giving and taking in equal amounts.

But not all stories come together as cinematically as Lizzie and Kathryn's did. One thing we're firm believers in that can help hedge against uncertainty: founder vesting. Think of it as a prenup for work wives. It assures that even if things end with a quickie divorce and hurt, the equity each partner holds reflects more than just the heart-eyed vibes of the honeymoon period. The concept is that cofounders (and early employees and advisers, if they're given a piece of the company) get their shares over time and not all at once, right out of the gate. It seems pretty obvious that a cofounder who leaves after a few months shouldn't get the same monetary return as one who stays with the company for years. But an equity windfall from the start sets up just that scenario. Investors love this slow roll because it helps ensure talent will stay right where they want it (working hard at the helm). In fact, many have even started to demand a founder vesting schedule before committing to funding.

Thinking about all of this contingency planning when things are just getting started can feel pretty grim. A lot of cofounders probably think, "If we have to have that conversation, we shouldn't be starting a business together, and since we're starting a business together . . . well, let's not have that conversation." But yes, the conversation has to happen. We were lucky that we never had to fall back on the cold comfort of vesting terms: We didn't deal with a horrific health crisis, no one had to move back home to tend to a sick parent, and neither of us experienced a sudden sense that the entrepreneurial life wasn't one she wanted. But we had a vesting schedule in place because the legal minds to whom we gave lots of (a) money and (b) trust said we had to—and because all sorts of unplannable things happen in life. People leave companies for lots of predictable and unpredictable reasons.

Okay, so back to our own equity tale: As time went on, our share breakdown proved to have no bearing on how we ran the business daily. We both had equal say in things, and neither of us *acted* or *felt* like she owned things more than the other. The percentages were just numbers on documents filed away in Dropbox somewhere. We seemed to have stumbled into a best-case scenario.

Those documents weren't something we thought about much in our day-to-day life . . . until they were. Several years into the business, after many unsuccessful attempts at fundraising, we suddenly had a term sheet on the table: A motley crew of old white dudes wanted to give us a lot of dollars . . . in exchange for 30 percent of the company. It wasn't a percentage either of us was comfortable with, and Erica pointed out that if we said yes, we'd be giving them as much ownership as she had. What had once been an amorphous number suddenly had a shape, a form. We ended up turning down their offer, but not before Claire had reassessed her positioning on the whole equity thing: If this was the type of math (and sacrifice) we'd be up against as we sought out additional investment for the business, it seemed only fair for Erica to own a bigger piece of the pie before it got sliced up and handed out to virtual strangers with fat checkbooks. A conversation that was full of unknowns only three years before was suddenly full of knowns, the most important one being that we were very much in this together for the long haul—and very much as equals.

Walking away from that investment offer—something we were able to do because the company was cash-flow positive at that point—remains one of the most powerful and prideful moments in the history of Of a Kind. There were lots of reasons for saying no—they wanted too much equity and too much involvement, we weren't sure they actually understood the business, and one of them would regularly call after 9 P.M. and leave voicemails that opened with "Hi, it's your boyfriend." But had we been in more desperate need of the funds, it's hard to say whether we'd have turned them down. Our financial wins had given us some degree of autonomy, and that felt like success.

On Making Financial Decisions Together

Getting comfortable navigating money—and understanding the way personal experiences, feelings, and vulnerabilities intersect with it—really starts to pay off when the big business questions come into play. For Anayvette Martinez and Marilyn Hollinquest of Radical Monarchs, aligning on money matters came naturally. "Both of us are very conservative with our cash because of the way we grew up financially. We're both from cash-poor families who worked super, super, super hard. Because we both have that background, we're very cautious with money," Marilyn says. When, three years post-launch in November 2017, they scored a big-deal grant from the NoVo Foundation, funded by Berkshire Hathaway shares supplied by Warren Buffett himself, they suddenly had the resources to dedicate themselves full time to growing their organization and its mission to support young girls' education in social justice and self-empowerment. This has meant having conversations about making significant investments, like adding staff, and smaller but important ones, like producing branded merch. The fact that these two are starting from a shared philosophy around money makes these discussions easier, even if they don't always start from a place of agreement. Says Marilyn: "We've definitely had multiple opportunities where we've had to have conversations around how we spend money. I think it's a back-and-forth of hearing each other's perspective and then saying, 'Okay, that makes sense.'"

In our case, after running Of a Kind for five years, we started to ponder a major financial decision of our own: acquisition. Selling the business wasn't a plan we'd had from the start, but we'd gotten tired of banging our heads against the wall to try to solve the same old problems of reaching a bigger audience, expanding our brand, and just straight-up scaling without access to enough resources or solutions. Over the course of the first half decade of the company, whenever we tested a new marketing scheme or expanded the product mix on our site, it came with a scary, potentially business-threatening financial risk, and the stress of wondering if and when money would run out left us facing burnout in a big way. When we sank thousands of dollars into advertising consulting services and saw zero return, we were suddenly looking at a drastically shorter runway for the life of our business. Sure, we'd prided ourselves on being scrappy, but at some point that became exhausting, and we could express that to each other without fear of being judged for it.

So we started having conversations with a few companies about what exactly acquisition might look like when applied to what we'd built, and in the summer of 2015, we sold Of a Kind to Bed Bath & Beyond. It was, to put it mildly, unexpected: Claire wore leather shorts to our first get-together with their team, a sartorial risk one takes only if she knows better than to get her hopes up about the outcome of any meeting. Something that helped put us at ease when it came to our BB&B sit-down is that we doubted it would be a conversation about acquisition. We walked into the room assuming they were interested in, at best, a retail partnership featuring some of the independent-design brands we work with or, at worst, an opportunity to pick our brains. But standing in the shiny elevator bank postmeeting, we turned to each other with the same bemused-but-excited looks on our faces: We liked them? Like, a lot? They respected what we'd built in five short years, understood our vision, and seemed to have a similar sensibility when it came to the basic principles of running a business—our companies were almost spookily aligned in ways we never would've guessed, right down to the founded-by-two-friends origin story. (A year later, we sat down with the BB&B founders to record an episode of our podcast about what it's like to start a company with your best pal—forty-plus years in, they had a few things to teach us.)

When we gathered around conference room tables with the Bed Bath & Beyond crew for follow-up conversations, we were honest about the struggles and failings we'd experienced through the years, the ways we thought we could benefit from their know-how, and where, in turn, we could lend our own savvy. We were articulate about what was important to us: that if Of a Kind became part of Bed Bath & Beyond, we'd be able to maintain the authenticity that was core to the brand and, furthermore, core to our job satisfaction. We also made the nature of our partnership clear and emphasized the importance of preserving it. By then, we knew full well how valuable it was to the company and how obvious our bond was to most who encountered us. Then, just three months and change after that initial meeting, we closed a deal that meant 100 percent of our company now belonged to *another* company. We went from Claire and Erica, business owners, to Claire and Erica, cofounders with a boss—who also didn't have to worry about where Of a Kind's next investment would come from. Trade-offs!

The acquisition decision that felt very right to us never did for the founders of Hanky Panky, though not for lack of opportunity. In 2004, when *The Wall Street Journal* ran a front-page story about Gale Epstein and Lida Orzeck's booming underwear business, demand went wild, putting pressure on their fifty-five-person, largely self-funded company to ramp up production fast. Stores were quickly selling out of their 4811 thong, a style that, the article noted, was favored by Cindy Crawford and Julianne Moore. "I was so overwhelmed," Lida says to Gale. "You must remember this: When we were walking uptown through the park, I said I thought I wanted out. We could've sold in a second." Instead, they pushed through the growth period, nearly tripling their headcount without a partner or outside investors, driven by, as Lida says, "a sense of loyalty to our employees and their communities and also the environmental impact it would have meant to go offshore." They knew that for a product like theirs, selling the company would mean taking production outside the United States, which would increase their carbon footprint considerably, have them traveling the globe, and leave much of their staff unemployed. It wasn't something they wanted for their brand, their customers, their team, or themselves. Their shared commitment to environmental sustainability, to those who worked for them, and to their lifestyle made it a clear decision. Their unified vision for how their company should operate allowed them to maintain full financial control. Then, on Hanky Panky's fortieth anniversary in 2017, with both women in their seventies, they opted to give some of it up: "We had to think about ways to create our exit eventually," Lida says. They set up an employee stock option plan, or ESOP, that transferred ownership of the company from the founders to a trust that benefits workers at their Manhattan HQ and their warehouse in Queens who have achieved a certain tenure. It's something they had been plotting—together—for a good ten years.

On Equal Accountability

Getting on the same page about making big money moves is easier when no one's in the dark about the state of the books. Sherry Jhawar and Allison Statter, the talent-and-brand matchmakers behind Blended Strategy Group, take a co-ownership approach to finances. "Sherry has led the charge in teaching me what it takes to run a business financially, like what benchmarks are good, what benchmarks are bad," Allison says. "But we sit down once or twice a month and look at our projections and talk about areas we want to grow in and how that affects our P&L." Sherry adds, "With the financials, it's really important that we talk it through: If we're going to do this, this is what this does to the business, and let's just both know it and go in holding hands and jumping in." They embrace the transparency that is core to their relationship when thinking about any investment—whether it's adding a headcount to facilitate a new client project or signing the lease on their "really cute but small" office. As Sherry says, "If something's falling apart, we talk about it right away. If something's going great, we talk. We talk about all of it just to make sure the other is aware so that if it turns into a fire, it's not like, 'Where did that fire come from, and how did I not know?'"

One such fire ignited on our watch while we were going through the wildly exciting, extraordinarily difficult process of selling the business. Due diligence is no joke, and it involved producing paperwork and an explanation for just about every business decision we'd ever made, including the ones we'd made when we had no clue what we were doing. It was one of the many moments when we found ourselves tremendously grateful that we'd had the good sense to hire lawyers and accountants from day one. But despite having had trained professionals on retainer since the moment we incorporated, we still had some serious errors to contend with during this phase. As it turned out, our longtime accountants had screwed up financial calculations in ways that were maddening and had deal-threatening consequences. Even in those stomach-churning, fist-shaking moments of discovering this screwup, we benefited greatly from a facet of our partnership that had been present from day one: equivalent amounts of financial visibility and accountability. We'd both always been equally scared of getting on the wrong side of the IRS, the State of New York, or another daunting government entity, and we were both quick to admit this vulnerability. So not only did we hire professionals, but we also *both* engaged routinely in regular check-ins around these topics, even when doing so felt like the least pressing, revenue-driving thing on our to-do lists. As much as we'd embraced a divide-and-conquer approach, we determined that the biggest, most critical aspects of a business shouldn't fall on just one set of shoulders when there were two sets available. An important call with the lawyer? We were both on it. A quarterly review of profit-and-loss statements with the accountants? The two of us attended together. Then, when the shit hit the fan, we'd both had equal distance from and equal visibility into the effed-up spreadsheets. Meaning, critically, that there was zero finger-pointing at each other—just at those accountants. Don't get us wrong: It was awful. It was anxiety-inducing. But there was nothing we could do, and—spoiler alert—we survived to tell the tale.

Once we'd waded through the paperwork, climbed out of the rage cage that sloppy bookkeeping built, and officially linked up with BB&B, we were surprised by the immediate effects that the erasure of certain financial pressures had on our psyches and the way that we ran a company together. By then, we'd become so accustomed to there never being enough money that we hadn't fully grasped how the responsibilities of making payroll and being accountable for other people's incomes had worn away at us. Or how draining it had been to be wildly undercompensated for a half decade.

This, like every other financial milestone we'd experienced as a pair, was emotional. Throughout our years running the show together, money had been the driving force behind tough talks, chest-clenchy meetings, tears, and many sleepless nights. It had also been the impetus for bonding sessions, high-fives, and moments when we felt like full-blown businesswoman successes. Money is weird, and it is also what you make of it. In any business partnership, it's a tie that binds—one that's strengthened when interactions around it are rooted in compassion, equality, and authenticity. We're not going to go so far as to say that we learned how to have fun with financials, but we learned how to get into the nitty-gritty of budgets and term sheets and, in all cases, to sign our names side by side on the dotted lines.

Surviving the Rough Patches

If I murdered someone, she's the person I'd call to help me drag the corpse across the living room floor. She's my person.

—CRISTINA YANG, *GREY'S ANATOMY*

O f all the work wives we spoke to for this book, very few fessed up to fighting. According to Leah Sheppard, a gender researcher and assistant professor of management at Washington State University, who's studied same-sex conflict among women in the workplace, at least some of this avoidance has roots in the ethos of female empowerment and solidarity: "You tend to hear women saying, 'We need to stick together. We shouldn't tear each other down,' which I agree with," she explained. "It's coming from a good place, but ultimately, I think these notions shape our perception so much that we start to view women offering criticism to other women as women undermining other women."

In her research, Leah found that we're far more critical of women who criticize other women than we are of men who criticize women. For example, in one experiment, Leah and another researcher had participants read about one of three workplace conflicts. The conflicts were identical, only the gendered names were different, so participants were either reading about a conflict between two men, two women, or a man and a woman. The study participants were then asked a series of questions to determine whether they thought the conflict would create long-term issues for the individuals involved and for the company. The findings? Female-female conflict was evaluated as "more problematic" than the other two types. In the resulting paper, they write, "Women might produce or exacerbate the negative consequences that stem from their same-sex conflict simply by holding the expectation that such conflict will be particularly dramatic and difficult to resolve."

In our experience, these biases against fighting tend to be compounded by a well-intentioned desire to present a united front and to put ego aside for the greater good. As Jessica Morgan of *Go Fug Yourself* explains it, "Some people love to fight. That's not how our relationship works, and I think both of us would rather come to a mutually agreeable compromise than win." Or, as her partner, Heather Cocks, puts it, "We would rather be rock stars than be right."

We aren't big fighters either, though it's not something we necessarily take pride in—at least anymore. Solidarity has always come to us naturally, but arguing was something we struggled with when we started working together—and, in this case, "struggled with" means "just didn't do." That's not to say that we never disagreed, never annoyed the crap out of each other, or never plain got sick of spending so much time with each other. It's just that when we did, we didn't do so communicatively. We bottled things up, shut down, and, more often than was healthy, told ourselves "Those are just *my* feelings. I should ignore them."

There were myriad reasons for this unspoken embargo on arguments early on. We had both, independently, convinced ourselves that there was basically no time in our busy work schedules for it. We had this idea that getting into a spat would ruin more than just the moments we'd spend hashing it out and thought that hurt feelings would derail the entire day. Because how do two people walk into a meeting unified after they've just gotten into it with each other? How does a person spend eight more hours with someone when they feel like they really need their space? And because we were actively avoiding doing it—except for, oh, once a year or so when it would all come pouring out in a weepy, not entirely constructive manner—we had no reason to assume that our fears were anything other than founded.

Back then, we were terrified that one fight would ruin *everything*. But while a friendship may be able to last a lifetime without any major disagreements, a successful business partnership requires a willingness to deal directly with dissent and frustration. If we had to point to one area in which the tensions between the norms of female friendship and the requirements of a business partnership butt up against each other, conflict avoidance is most certainly it. As friends, we hadn't ever been forced to learn to deal with discord or tension between us, but making the transition to work wives meant determining how to broach it.

On Learning to Fight

When it came to our own conflict style (or lack thereof), we sensed we were doing it (or, erm, not doing it) all wrong, and our management coach confirmed that when we started seeing him. Right away, he made it clear to us that we had to start articulating our feelings when we were annoyed, frustrated, or just straight-up mad at the other. "Brittle things break," he said. He encouraged us to add arguing to our relationship repertoire so that it wasn't such a big, scary deal. According to him, the point is not to scream and yell at each other but to air our grievances, regularly and comfortably. And then to let those things go: Have the contained disagreement, and then move on. Developing this skill was and is a work in progress. The string of disagreements that followed took place almost exclusively in cars because it meant we didn't have to look at each other while we hashed them out. (This, by the way, is a very useful tactic for argument-averse individuals, and it works just as well during a walk as it does during a drive.) Though we're grateful to have had the push from a professional to get us there, we would have benefited greatly from getting comfortable in combat way earlier on in our partnership.

If positioning conflict as a core component of a healthy business partnership seems odd, consider its role within other intimate relationships: "Except for the sex, founders have the same interdependency as married couples," Peter Pearson of the Couples Institute in Menlo Park, California, told *The New York Times*. And we all know the short shelf life of couples who claim they never fight—it's the ones who know how to get into it with each other, but also how to get over it and not go to bed pissed, that last. As experts and seasoned work partners are quick to point out, not fighting is *not* a sign of relationship health. It's much better to practice early when the stakes are lower rather than waiting for extreme turmoil to hit. The goal is to get good at battling it out productively so that when things get really hard, the tools are at the ready.

But no matter how much practice a person gets, initiating a tough conversation is never the most appealing item on a to-do list. One thing that helped us? Developing regular routines that make the time and space for these conversations, like a weekly check-in—which, by the way, is something we didn't officially do for years. That sounds insane—we know—but when you spend your days sitting across from each other, it also sounds slightly nutty to suggest carving out more time to . . . sit across from each other. And yet! Setting a regular appointment means having a designated time to deal with shit, good and bad. It does away with the excuse we'd frequently given to ourselves: that there was no right time to bring something up. It also gives us an opportunity to ensure we're aligned on things happening in the business or to deal with it if we're not.

We often close out our one-on-ones with the question "How are you feeling about everything?"—an extraordinarily useful conversation to have, regardless of whether there's friction. It's an effective device for opening up a tough conversation without an emotional dump or, worse, an accusation. More often than not, if one of us is feeling frustrated, the other is, too, and it'll usually come up in response to that question. Sometimes the approach is more direct, sending a "Do you have 10 min to talk this AM?" Slack message, a bat-signal that something has surfaced that we need to squash. Whatever the method, more in-the-moment quarreling has given us the realization that we have a plenty strong foundation on which to argue without thwarting a day's agenda.

We're not the only ones who've gotten more adept at making room for conflict along the way. In the beginning of their partnership, Amanda Hesser and Merrill Stubbs of Food52 tried not to bring feelings to the office at all—because what did their fears and anxieties have to do with recipe-testing, selling ad deals, or establishing an editorial calendar, really? Well, it turns out, *everything.* "We were bottling some things up because, in the early phase, it felt inappropriate to share personal anxieties in a work setting—which is so ridiculous now when I look back on it," Amanda says. But once they started opening up, it was like taking the lid off a pressure cooker. "The minute we started putting this stuff out there, that just changed everything," Merrill explains. "It allowed us to release the tension by verbalizing it to the other person, and then if they weren't feeling the same, which is pretty often the case, you feel this relief." Getting to this emotionally open place meant confronting the nature and scope of the relationship they were forging. "It's hard to actually own up to how deep a commitment it is when you start a company," says Amanda, acknowledging that she and Merrill are more than colleagues, Food52 is more than a job, and the turmoil they experience together takes up more space as a result.

These two are quick to identify the crucial element in their relationship that allows them to argue with ease: They trust that both they—and their relationship—are tough enough to handle whatever issues come up. "Sometimes when I'm feeling anxious, my first thought is, 'I don't want to make Merrill feel like this.' If she's feeling good, I don't want to burden her," Amanda explains. "But I think we've gotten better at seeing that we're both strong, and we can handle hard news from the other person." Not presuming the worst-case outcome is key, Merrill points out: "I think sometimes when you go into a hard conversation, the assumption is that you're going into battle. We trust each other so much now that, going into a hard conversation of any kind—whether it's revealing anxiety or expressing our frustration—we both understand that the other person is going to receive it from a place of wanting to work through it. Because we have had so many of them now, we've exercised those muscles, and it makes it so much easier because we know what the other one wants: We want each other to be happy, to succeed, to feel good."

Knowing how dedicated each is to the other means they can express concerns directly, and they can also be vulnerable without fearing that it's a show of weakness. Vulnerability, typically lauded in the context of personal relationships—particularly female ones—tends to get a bad rap in an office environment. But discouraging it also shuts out qualities like courage and honesty that attend it—which ultimately does a disservice to businesses. Dr. Brené Brown, an expert on the topic, defines vulnerability as "the willingness to be 'all in' even when you know it can mean failing and hurting" and positions it as "the birthplace of joy, belonging, creativity, authenticity, and love." Which is to say: It's the source of some very positive emotions that we want to both bring to work and derive from work. Merrill cited a recent feelings fest as evidence of how this plays out for them: "The other week, we were like, 'Let's hop on the phone to talk about this thing'—because there was a flood of emails that had gone back and forth about something timely that we didn't see eye to eye on, and the tension was mounting. We ended up both crying on the phone. And it was not planned in any way—it was like, 'Uh, we're feeling this way. Let's just deal with it, like, right now.'" By having these interactions often enough that they feel routine instead of scary, the Food52 founders have opened up the space for both turmoil and tears in their relationship, whenever either comes up. This in turn has paved the way for qualities like candor and contentment to live at the center of their working relationship.

None of this is to suggest that fighting is ever easy—even for those who have a higher comfort level with it or, as Merrill puts it, those who've "exercised those muscles" over and over. It's especially thorny when the point of conflict feels inherently tied to someone's sense of self. That management coach of ours, Dr. Ben Michaelis, sees a lot of cofounders, work wives, business buds, and married couples. His take: "It's very challenging to be in a relationship where you have dual roles." In any partnership, work or romantic, the needs of the two people involved are theoretically in line, but when something else enters the mix—like a second function as parent or a boss—things get complicated.

"When you have a business together, it's sort of like having a child," he explains. "Your needs aren't necessarily aligned, because if you think the child needs *this* kind of parenting, and your partner thinks the child needs *that* kind of parenting, conflict emerges." When, as managers, we feel like two moms navigating how to discipline the kids, Claire more naturally falls into the role of hardass when the situation calls for it, but she gets tired of feeling like the bad cop. Knowing that this has caused strife in the past, Erica is more conscious of stepping up as an enforcer for the sake of our twosome.

"As businesses develop, you get into all sorts of issues that tend to come up with couples, such as jealousy around who's seen as the leader, who's seen as the more competent one," Dr. Michaelis adds. "Things can get really, really hairy there because that's where a lot of issues from childhood tend to emerge, where you're like, 'Well, I was always seen as the pretty one,' or 'I was always seen as the smart one . . . ' And so these issues of identity end up getting really tangled and murky. There's a lot of work around trying to define what each member of the dyad wants to be and then also assessing their capacities."

Volleyball powerhouse Kerri Walsh Jennings is quick to identify how her own childhood shaped her conflict-spiking approach: "I'm from a very big family—very no excuses, suck it up, don't complain. That's how I was raised, and that's my mode of operating." But that approach didn't work when she partnered with Misty May-Treanor, whose father, Butch, was prone to giving his daughter—and her playing partners— ample (and often critical) feedback on their game. Dealing with assessments from Misty's dad left Kerri feeling powerless and unsure of how—or who—to confront: "I remember talking to Misty at one point, being like, 'Misty, can you please just stand up for me? This hurts me,' " Kerri recalls. "She said, 'Kerri, I can't change it. I don't even hear it.' That helped me—it helped me stop blaming Misty." Eventually, Kerri took up her frustration with Butch directly and felt better for it. Kerri echoed what we—and the Food52 duo—came to realize when we broke our own seal on bickering. "A confrontation doesn't always mean a fight, and I certainly learned that," she says. "Now I appreciate the intimacy that comes from conflict, to a certain extent."

On Learning What's Worth Fighting About

Though we're hardcore champions of getting comfortable with confrontation, we're *not* making a case for going head to head over every little thing. Our own early days of not fighting did help us learn what was worth arguing about at all. By never hashing it out with each other until things had simmered down and boiled up again and again, we learned what would pass . . . and what wouldn't. We have a better sense now of the things that create ongoing tension for us—hiring new people who aren't yet tuned in to our dynamic, taking on new projects that throw off our creativity-and-workload balance. We're trying to be better about getting ahead of that stuff—of seeing the red flag when it's half-mast rather than when it's flapping in the breeze.

That's something Deb Baker and Barbara Diner of Higher Standard Packaging had to work through: When they first launched their cannabis company, Barbara spearheaded the majority of the outreach to their vendors, and Deb didn't have the sense of ownership she wanted . . . in the business she co-owned. "I was feeling more like a secretary than I was feeling like a managing partner," Deb explains. The foundation for this tension stemmed from the independence they relished in their preretirement careers. Deb was a teacher who commanded a classroom, and Barbara was a marketing consultant—and they'd both enjoyed relative autonomy and weren't used to sharing the reins. The solve was a simple one: They talked about it, voiced their respective concerns, and split the vendor list in half. That doesn't meant they don't still have to remind themselves to put the business ahead of their feelings from time to time. "I'm learning how to take a step back and say, 'This isn't about power. This isn't about who's right or who's wrong. This is what's best for our company. So stop it, Deb—you're acting like you're seven or something,'" Deb explains. "I mean, I still catch myself."

On Picking Up Signals

The mantra that Deb's partner, Barbara, applies to her partnership is the same piece of advice she's given to friends about romantic partners for years: "They're not mind readers. Don't wait around for them to figure it out. Just tell them what you need, tell them what it looks like, tell them what it smells like, tell them what you want. Don't set them up for failure." Though Barbara's right about speaking up and being direct, we all tend to rely on a certain amount of nonverbal communication—navigating passive-aggressive body language and knowing when to ignore unspoken signals entirely is all part of the communication matrix, too. But if a relationship depends heavily on IMs, texts, and emails (and, let's be honest, GIFs and emoji), then learning what topics are worth wresting from the tonal ambiguity of thumbed communications is key. That's a quandary that the Call Your Girlfriend threesome navigates on the regular, given the bicoastal nature of their partnership. "There have been cases where one of us has to say, 'I don't like having a conversation like this on email. Let's save it for the next phone call,'" explains Ann Friedman.

And even better than a phone call? An in-person hang, preferably poolside in caftans in Palm Springs. Explains her partner Aminatou Sow of the impetus for their first retreat, "Well, for one, it was an opportunity to have a vacation. There were too many horses in the barn, and we just needed to talk about it." Adds Ann, "I think we were pretty burned out. There were a few awkward, difficult decision-making processes that spoke to the fact that we hadn't had some of these bigger conversations."

Though they didn't necessarily intend for it to be an annual occurrence when they first descended on the desert, they ended up staging a revival the next year so they could once again step back and think bigger-picture—and address any hang-ups that had been gnawing at them since they last converged. Taking time away from the grind to think macro, vent in a safe space, and, hey, just be friends for a sec feels like a worthwhile practice even for same-state work wives. In fact, it's something the women behind Radical Monarchs have done at least once a year since starting their nonprofit: At their first retreat, Anayvette Martinez and Marilyn Hollinquest established their organization's operating principles, and at each one since, they've set an agenda to reflect on the previous year and goal-set for the one ahead. But there's always good food and pool time, too. Says Anayvette, "We do mani-pedis and bring our spa stuff, so it's balanced."

As Anayvette and Marilyn know, getting quality face time can be tough even in the same city. Jessica Morgan and Heather Cocks of *Go Fug Yourself* have been living that L.A. life as long

as they've worked together. But, like true Angelenos, they re-
fuse to navigate the 405, even for each other. Instead of par-
taking in the freeway madness, they each work separately
from home, brainstorming their blog's awards-season cover-
age or workshopping the outline of a new novel over instant
messages and emails. They get together IRL only about once
a month. We were dumbfounded when they revealed this to
us, but, then again, they've been at it since 2004, so maybe
they're on to something. Their Gchat exchanges are longer
than the books they write, and they've become particularly
adept at parsing the particularities of internet dialogue or, as
importantly, learning how *not* to read tone into their typed
missives at all. If someone's actually upset about something,
it's on her to voice it, right? That's the assumption these two
are operating under. Exhibit A, according to Jessica: "We had
a conversation recently where I was like, 'We need to agree
that when we say things like "How's the book outline going?"
it's not like "Where the fuck is it?" It's "No, seriously, I'm just
curious."' Because that is such a loaded question." And, as if
words aren't hard enough to interpret, there are the periods,
question marks, and exclamation points to contend with.
"Heather has said to me in the past, 'I can tell you're in a bad
mood because of the punctuation marks,'" Jessica explains.
"I'm never mad at her—I'm just in a bad mood." Still, since
they can't see each other's faces or hear their voices, they have
to resist the urge to overanalyze what is presented to them. "I
can tell that it's not going well when Jessica types, 'Okay period,'" Heather says.

Per the linguist Deborah Tannen, these subtle but substantial cues are a form of indirectness "whereby meaning is not explicit in words but nonetheless comes across loud and clear" that's a common device women in the United States employ when trying to send a message, and it's actually rooted in a desire to be considerate and likable while doing so. As Tannen learned, other women are especially adept at interpreting this form of indirectness, and it can actually have real benefits. She writes: "The satisfaction of conversations like this—knowing that your meaning came across without your having to hammer it home, and that you've accurately interpreted another's meaning, is one of the great pleasures of women's friendship, when they have similar conversational styles. It's like a verbal pas de deux." And, we'd add, it creates an especially great advantage in the workplace, where communication is everything. Jessica says of Heather's meaning-laden punctuation: "I've learned to be like, 'It's not at me.' And if it's at me, she'll tell me it's at me." It's worth noting that no one we talked with for this book suggested airing serious grievances over instant message, WhatsApp, or any other tone-challenged communication channels. That's what phone calls, drives across the 405, or weekend offsites are for.

On Shared Adversaries

While we—and most of the work wives we interviewed—still have some progress to make when it comes to openly expressing frustration with each other, we've always found great success in turning our collective ire outward—toward others and the world at large. Maybe it's a by-product of coming of age during the era of *Daria* and Alanis Morissette—or maybe it's just that being part of a team fuels this us-against-the-world animosity. Either way, we'd argue there's something productive about it. We'll call it the "common-enemy effect," and it goes something like this: Want to quickly move past an argument with somebody? Put a nagging annoyance in perspective? Feel bonded in a moment of struggle? Simply direct that negative energy toward a common enemy! Try it and see.

One particularly illuminating instance: During our third attempt to raise money from VCs—something we were (1) terrible and (2) unsuccessful at—there was a particularly memorable subway ride. It followed a couple dozen investor meetings, so much equivocation (no one says yes *or* no, infuriatingly), and too much time spent in heels. We were shoulder to shoulder, slouched in an over-air-conditioned MTA car, staring straight ahead and saying so much by not talking at all. Claire broke the silence with, "Do you want to quit Of a Kind? I understand if you do. I just don't know how anyone else could be masochistic enough to keep doing this."

These are the conversations we've always been good at having: When things get hard, we huddle closer together, like we are DIYing our own little bomb shelter and preparing for the fallout. (We'd have such great snacks.) Outside forces trying to stomp us out make us clutch each other tighter. In their weird way, these low points can reinvigorate our partnership and—triteness, coming through!—remind us what really matters. As Kerri Walsh Jennings explains of going for gold with Misty May-Treanor, having an adversary helps unify: "We developed this partnership where, really early on in our career, we had a huge target on our backs because we were one of the best right away. I came to cherish that because it was like we were united against the world, and that really created such a big, strong bond." The common enemy: Sometimes it comes in the form of a power-hungry, time-wasting herd of venture capitalists, and sometimes it comes in the form of a victory-crazed army of Olympic athletes.

On Hard Times

According to one theory, this cling-to-each-other reaction to tough times is more than just a tic—it's a response that's downright ingrained in women. In the late nineties, Shelley E. Taylor, a psychology professor at UCLA, took a closer look at the widely accepted and understood primal instinct of fight-or-flight when a postdoc student of hers noticed that animal stress studies were conducted using only male rats. Delving into similar published studies on humans, Taylor et al. found that before 1995, women made up only 17 percent of the subjects.

In a groundbreaking paper published in the *Psychology Review* in 2000, Taylor and her colleagues offered a new theory: "We propose that human female responses to stress (as well as those of some animal species) are not well characterized by fight-or-flight, as research has implicitly assumed, but rather are more typically characterized by a pattern we term 'tend-and-befriend.' Specifically, we suggest that, by virtue of differential parental investment, female stress responses have selectively evolved to maximize the survival of self and offspring. We suggest that females respond to stress by nurturing offspring, exhibiting behaviors that protect them from harm and reduce neuroendocrine responses that may compromise offspring health (the tending pattern), and by befriending, namely, affiliating with social groups to reduce risk." Basically: Women, unlike men, don't respond to stress by getting combative or bolting—instead, we nurture, protect, and bond, all in the name of survival. That said: Taylor's theory is predicated on an essentialist narrative steeped in a biological definition of womanhood that starts to fall apart when viewed through a more contemporary understanding of gender, a social construct. But like it or not (and we don't), it's also hard to ignore that even the most modern notions of socially conditioned femininity are strongly tied to the role of motherhood that this theory places front and center.

In a business setting, where dilemmas present themselves on a daily basis, the tendency toward tend-and-befriend is a tremendous boon. It means a willingness not only to hunker down and address issues head-on but also to care for and soothe one another as part of the process. It provides a framework for solving problems, safeguarding relationships, and prioritizing self-care. Pamela Koffler and Christine Vachon of Killer Films put this notion to the test in a big way when, in 2008, their stress responses were turned up to eleven: In ex-

tremely short succession, Pam had a baby, Christine was diag-
nosed with breast cancer, Pam's mom died, and then boom:
the financial crisis. The economic downturn wasn't great for
any industry, but film was especially hard-hit, and the conflu-
ence of all of this shittiness forced them to question just how
much, exactly, they were willing to do for each other and for
their business. Things got very dark very fast, and part of Killer's survival was rooted in who Christine and Pam were and
are: the sort of women willing to stick it out through the bad
times and ones who, as Pam puts it, recognize that "this partnership is offering us both more of what we do want and need
out of life and work than not."

Beyond the grit and tenacity that anchored their relationship lay some textbook tend-and-befriend behavior. When circumstances pulled them each into their own separate black
holes, away from each other and away from the company
they'd built, survival instincts kicked in. "I do remember one
really crystal-clear moment that may be the culmination of
this tough time: Christine was in Sweden, and she got her di-
agnosis during that big trip," Pam says. "I had an infant, it
was less than a year after my mom died, and our bank account
got frozen. I realized, okay, I have to deal with this. Christine
can't. This is serious. She is about to go into chemo and radiation, and there are no choices anymore. This person needs my
support. The company needs a practical problem solved. Get
the fuck over yourself and show up. I really remember that
feeling, and it was almost a relief."

Eventually, the Killer team found financial stability by

landing a major deal with HBO to produce a miniseries called *Mildred Pierce*. But Christine's radiation treatments prevented her from taking the lead in the ways she otherwise would have on this particular project. A major health crisis timed with a business-reviving opportunity left no room for hand-wringing when it came to Pam's role: "It was just so clear: 'Christine cannot do this, and this is big. I can, so I will.'" It was suddenly very obvious how to show up and be the partner she needed to be—a lesson they both say has helped them understand how to better serve each other even when shit *isn't* hitting the fan. As Pam explains it, "In some ways, those very concrete parameters that are unambiguous really helped. Then you do it when it becomes more optional and discretionary. I guess we got lucky that there were those storms of circumstances that didn't completely undermine everything but gave us the path forward." Christine adds: "We also started to figure out strategies. I think what we both, to some degree, learned from this was you do have to give yourself a break."

It's hard not to walk away from these stories with a conviction that adversity strengthens a partnership. But what about when adversity leads to the dissolving of the partnership— and not by choice? After nearly a decade of helming *Lucky* magazine, Kim France and Andrea Linett left. As happens in the publishing industry, there was an unceremonious and abrupt changing of the guard. Eight years later, they still complete each other's sentences when retelling the tale:

KIM: I got fired on Rosh Hashanah.

ANDREA: My husband and I were in New Jersey going out to my mom's house because I always took the day off, but Kim never did—she is a bad Jew.

KIM: I texted her and said . . .

ANDREA: She goes, "Call me now."

KIM: "It is urgent that you call me back right away."

ANDREA: She goes, "I just got fired."

KIM: Andrea was like, "I guess this means I'm going to get fired, too." I was like, "It probably means you are going to get fired, too."

ANDREA: I think I waited three weeks before [the new editor], Brandon Holley, fired me. We talked every day. You were like, "Get out of there—just get the hell out of there." I was like, "No, I need my severance."

KIM: Which was right. She should stick around for her severance. It was a tense time. I didn't want to talk about it because I was out of there, and I was happy to be out of there. I was relieved. Yeah, it was weird. I mean, we still miss working together.

ANDREA: We had something we were working on, and then I don't know what happened. We had an idea. I think we should jump back on that.

Hearing Kim and Andrea talk about wanting to get back in the game as partners again was tremendously comforting to us. Having been at this for a while now—with ups and downs and moments that have felt like inflection points—we've had plenty of opportunities to wonder: Who would we be without the business? How would our relationship fare? Would our work-wife life be R.I.P.? Reassuringly, a good ways out from their departure from the magazine in 2010, Kim and Andrea are still Kim and Andrea. "We talk at least twice a day. We go for coffee, we putz around, we do the same things," Andrea says. Their relationship was wrapped up in the thing they built, but it wasn't contained by it.

The closest we've ever come to answering those "What if?" questions for ourselves was during one particularly struggle-laden stage when we thought Of a Kind was bound to go under—we'd spent too much of our time and our limited funding on a tech-intensive project that we thought would help us grow more quickly. We had our sights set on becoming a marketplace-style retailer, a move we hoped would allow us to sell a lot more stuff without having to increase the amount of inventory we were carrying on our books or in our ware-house. But in addition to being costly, it didn't play to our strengths: It required operational and logistical heavy lifting, areas of the business neither of us enjoy nor excel at. We found ourselves distracted from the day-to-day of running the company, focused instead on solving problems that failed to ignite passion in either of us. We were miserable and frus-trated, but we'd convinced ourselves it was the only way to scale. Unsurprisingly, the initiative didn't take, and we couldn't come up with a way out of this hole we'd dug.

In the midst of all this, we dragged our downtrodden selves

to a routine meeting with the founders of our then tech agency. Upon hearing us recount the various ways in which we were attempting to keep the company solvent, these two guys offered up an alternative: Scrap Of a Kind and come work with them on a startup concept they'd been wanting to launch. Their big idea? Selling secondhand footwear—but on the internet! Insert reaction GIF here. We turned them down on the spot—we had our wits about us, even during this state of extreme desperation. Instead of going back to the office after that meeting, we went to Claire's apartment and collapsed on her bed with our coats still on. We stared up at the ceiling and talked. Sure, we knew for certain that we did not want to helm a used-shoe empire, but what exactly *would* we want to do if Of a Kind were no more? What *was* important to us in this theoretical next chapter? The thing we kept coming back to was the necessity of keeping our twosomeness intact—of finding our footing again as a pair.

Our biz persevered—we put our heads down, muscled through this low point, and exhaled *deeply* when a big partnership opportunity surfaced that helped turn the tide. But there will inevitably be other valleys on our winding path to moguldom, and knowing we've got each other to lean on and even to respectfully quarrel with feels like one hell of a trust fall. We have a sense of security and a sense of priority—a clear framework from which to make decisions, make confessions, and just generally be a little more honest with ourselves and with each other. And we know that's worth fighting for.

Having Babies (Besides the Business)

I already know how to breathe, and I am the last
person who needs lessons on how to push.

—MURPHY BROWN, *MURPHY BROWN*

A whole chapter on babies? Yes, and here's why:
The inability of the American workplace to effectively adapt
to accommodate working parents remains one of the biggest
hurdles to women's professional advancement. And yet, as we
made our way through interviews with duos and trios of
women who'd navigated motherhood as both colleagues and
allies—and as business leaders—we witnessed arrangements
that transformed the experience for both working mothers
and their coworkers. These weren't policies put in place by
well-intentioned HR departments; they were acts of friend-

ship from one woman to another, meant to provide support during a vulnerable time. It struck us as one of the most potent examples of the work-wife effect: The qualities and instincts inherent in women's relationships, applied to workplace practices, are providing a critical foundation for the long-term health of businesses.

For our own part, one of the most emotional conversations we've ever had as friends or as business partners took place while we were driving from West Hollywood to Pasadena during a work trip in 2016, changing lanes, broaching the topic of having kids. Neither of us had any, Claire was pretty sure she wanted them but wondered how someone can ever be completely sure of something so *huge,* and Erica did not want any and had been certain of this for a decade. We'd been discussing those general POVs for a good long time, but it was a subject that we talked about primarily in hypothetical terms. Mostly we talked about the ways in which our choices affected our relationships with *other* people: our parents, our husbands, etc. Sure, we probably tossed around some mild ruminations about what it would mean for us and for our partnership—but nothing material or nuanced because, again: hypothetical. Suddenly, though, as we made our way into our thirties, and into Pasadena, this baby-having was looking less theoretical and more real.

A few times on this West Coast trip, Erica had made offhand comments about parenting quirks we'd both witnessed during meetings or drinks when babies had been in tow. It wasn't really anything new to our rapport. Erica, who'd had plenty of opportunities to defend her position on not wanting kids, as women in her position are so often (and so unfairly) forced to do, had developed a keen ability to zero in on the more humorous and arduous parts of parenting. But as Claire had begun to anticipate motherhood in more concrete ways, the comments carried new weight and started to feel like deeply personal—if deeply passive—commentary on her own intentions. She felt as if Erica was putting these new moms under a microscope—one Claire did not want to be under if/when she had her own progeny. It heightened her own insecurities around what it would be like to give birth to and raise a kid while running a business, having two partners, trying to keep her shit together.

Erica was totally taken aback by Claire's reaction. She thought she was just picking things apart, getting far too granular in the way that the two of us so often did. She hadn't considered Claire's on-the-precipice-of-potential-motherhood emotions. But she *had* put a good amount of thought (anxiety?) into how her own not having kids would become a defining feature as she got older—that she'd never bond with Claire (or anyone else) about colic or infant weight gain, preschool applications or speech development. Though she was cool with being Aunt Erica in theory, it was tough knowing that so very many of her friends would have this thing in common. In keeping with the theme of this meltdown, Claire had not considered—even for a moment—this particular downside of Erica's footloose-and-kiddie-free choice. She was too busy getting preemptively jealous of the unfettered access to sleep, the lack of need for a college savings fund, and the ability to stay at the office past preschool pickup time.

When we started to (a) cry a little and (b) unpack what we were feeling, we realized we were both scared of what could come during this era—for each of us individually and for us together. As Amanda Hesser reminded us in an earlier chapter, it's difficult to understate—and difficult to understand— what an enormous commitment it is to start a company together . . . and solving for how such a fundamental life change would figure into that equation felt uncharted and scary. We both fretted about being judged, being left behind, being the sort of lonely, forgotten parent or nonparent who just didn't Get It. We both wrung our hands about whether we'd be able to do our part to support each other in business and in life. How would this look, feel, smell when the time came? How would we know how to be? And, most importantly: How would this friendship, this partnership, this company—all of which were very much anchors of our lives and our livelihoods—fare? The only solid conclusions we came to were, as far as we're concerned, the most important ones: We're both on the same page about each other's intentions, and we're both committed to traversing each other's life milestones together.

On Navigating New Motherhood

For some real-talk and genuine strategies from women who've actually lived through the baby-having stages of work-wifing, look no further than Amanda Hesser and Merrill Stubbs of Food52. When they started their home cooking internet oasis, Amanda had twin toddlers, which put pressure on her in ways that Merrill admits she didn't really appreciate at the time. "Now that I am a parent and I understand it on a personal level, I think it must have been very challenging for Amanda to have kids and for me not to have kids early on," she explains. When she embarked on the journey to becoming a parent herself, the business was in full swing, and she and Amanda ran up against new hurdles in figuring out how to work through it. It was messy, it was emotional, and they didn't get it right right away. The first talk they had about Merrill's maternity leave was . . . rough. "Before I had my first child, there were so many question marks, and I was pretty panicky thinking about what it was going to mean and how I was going to feel," Merrill explains. "I wanted to have a maternity leave that felt real, and when I first told Amanda, she was like, 'What the hell?' I didn't know what parenthood was going to be like, and I was just terrified that I wasn't going have enough time to feel like I was doing it right, whatever that meant." Amanda wasn't being insensitive—her fear was just showing through. As Amanda puts it, "It's not that I didn't have empathy for her feelings. I was panicked about our partnership and Merrill's commitment. This company had to work. I was so deeply invested, and I was like, 'What do you mean you don't know when you want to come back?' I think I was like a deer in headlights."

Fortunately, this rocky beginning was not representative of

what followed. After Amanda had a couple days to process her feelings, they regrouped and, per Merrill, Amanda made an extremely touching apology to her that went something like this: "I want to revisit this conversation because I know that I was shocked, and I'm sure you felt that. Yes, I'm freaked out, but I want you to have time with the baby. If you don't, I don't want to regret that. I don't want to feel like I kept you from that." That talk, Merrill says, did wonders to put her at ease—both the stepping away and the coming back suddenly seemed more manageable.

When a partnership is as all-encompassing, meaningful, and life-changing as the kind that Merrill and Amanda have, it seems impossible for it not to feel threatened by something as, well, all-encompassing, meaningful, and life-changing as having a child. But being able to give each other the time and the space to have a newborn, to parent, to feel connected to this very big-deal life thing is an opportunity to strengthen the work-wife bond in the process, too. When Merrill was out with her first baby, she felt actively taken care of by Amanda, who sent her weekly email updates detailing everything important going down at the office while shielding her from all of the bullshit she didn't need to be distracted by. Amanda's status reports, which kept Merrill in the know without her having to be in the thick of it, were the extraordinarily generous act of a woman who knew from experience what would be useful in this scenario. But more than that, they're also a potentially game-changing convention. Imagine a world where this sort of thing—this sort of thinking in general—was customary practice for women on maternity leave. Would the number of mothers who opted not to return to work after their leave, daunted by so many factors, including the task of getting back up to speed, drop? And if and when they did return, would they be better positioned for advancement?

According to the *Harvard Business Review,* 43 percent of highly qualified women with kids leave the workplace for some period of time. What any ambitious woman knows is that for many working moms, this move is less about women choosing not to climb to the top and a whole lot more about feeling they have no choice but to step on the brakes—whether that's due to limited time, resources, money, or support.

Could the way Amanda handled Merrill's leave—spread across a whole swath of people—help thwart the motherhood penalty, which systematically puts women with kids behind in the workforce? It starts with pay, which, after childbirth, drops an average of 4 percent for every kid, but it extends to perceived competence, authority, and dependability. According to Michelle Budig, a sociology professor at the University of Massachusetts, men, on the other hand, get what's called a fatherhood bonus—and not just in the form of, on average, a 6 percent raise. "Employers read fathers as more stable and committed to their work; they have a family to provide for, so they're less likely to be flaky," she told *The New York Times.* When the Work, Family, and Health Network—a team of researchers brought together by the National Institutes of Health and the Centers for Disease Control and Prevention—published a guide to how businesses can support working families, one of the key recommendations was to build in management support for employees' personal lives—and Amanda and Merrill's weekly maternity leave updates feel like a shining example of just that. These two are proof that when women partner together in the workplace, these types of progressive shifts happen naturally.

Another case in point: Pamela Koffler and Christine Vachon of Killer Films built their business and their partnership in a way that made room for motherhood—quite literally at times. When their now-teenage kids were babies, Pam and Christine's company was in its own relative infancy. "I was very taken aback by how hard it was for me to leave the kid," Pam recalls. "I did try to wedge in as much time with the kid and work. It was made possible by an open attitude in our business and our partnership. Us saying, 'Let's have a crib in this little room,' or 'Let's do this conference call from home.' I took it day by day, chapter by chapter, and suddenly the toddler was in preschool." In having each other to turn to, Pam and Christine were able to partner on the logistics—they could figure things out together as issues came up and could land on solves like a BYO crib along the way. They could put their heads together about what meetings could be missed, what trips definitely couldn't. That they were able to do this so effectively speaks to the power of the feminine proclivity for collaboration and multitasking. And, of course, the fact that they were in charge and could make the call. As the bosses, they could create a workplace that suited them, their lives, and their experiences as women, and having done that is still serving them now. "I had such a hard day recently with my kids," Pam says. "I was just like, 'I'm going to my happy place now.' I'm gonna get to my desk, have my coffee. It's all problems I can solve, I'm good at, and I have Christine there. Life is good when you enjoy going to your desk every day. It's not some hideous, stressful, cutthroat, alienating experience, which I do think the corporate workplace is for so many people."

Having an ally who says "You can do this. We can do this"—whether she has a kid or not—is powerful. Especially when it's followed with a "Here's how." That gave Nicole van der Weerden more zeal as she took on the role of mother . . . at the same time as she took on the role of CEO at the biotech firm Hexima. "Other people were like, 'You'll have the baby, and then you'll be a mess, and you won't be able to do it,' " she says. Marilyn Anderson, her work wife (and the woman who recruited her into the position), had an alternative take: "No, you'll be okay if you plan for it." Marilyn, a grandmother who had witnessed her own daughter—a mother studying to be a surgeon—juggle it all, offered up the solutions she'd been a part of creating in her own family: "When my daughter had an important meeting when the baby was young, sometimes we would book a hotel room next to where the meeting was. My husband and I would babysit, and she'd run back and forth and feed. For our important Hexima meetings—the first time, Nicole's baby was only two weeks old—we did that. We rented a hotel room next to the meeting, Nicole's husband stayed there, and Nicole went back and forth." Marilyn knows firsthand what it looks like when women don't have this kind of supportive professional environment: She gave birth to her first child during her postdoctoral fellowship, and there was no maternity leave available to her. "That was appalling," she says. "I didn't want Nicole to go through that." Marilyn and Nicole talked out these tactics before Nicole took the C-suite job and, more importantly, well before Nicole gave birth.

The support Marilyn extended to Nicole as she took on motherhood included encouraging Nicole to take work-from-home days, claiming that, all things considered, she'd likely be more productive than if she were at the office with a whole team of employees seeking her attention. When the arrival of a newborn leads to a general loosening of the reins—a WFH Friday, a bring-the-baby-to-work day here and there, a meeting done by phone instead of in-person—that less rigid structure is likely to benefit the entire office. A 2016 study on tech employees published in the *American Sociological Review* found that when workers had a voice in their schedules, they had lower levels of stress and higher job satisfaction. Flexibility: It's not just for parents.

On Figuring In Partnership

The importance of developing tactics and coping mechanisms to make way for a new baby is a given—but what of the tactics and coping mechanisms for the partnership itself? It's a funny and amazing thing to go through a milestone like this with an adult who does not sleep in your bed, but whose livelihood is seriously impacted all the same. It's expected that a person would discuss plans for procreation with her domestic partner, if she has one—ideally at great length before doing it. But what does that talk look like when it comes to a business partner?

Not being communicative about big life changes well in advance can make it hard to know how to really be there for a person, something that pro volleyball player Misty May-Treanor experienced firsthand when she felt blindsided by the pregnancy of her playing partner Kerri Walsh Jennings, who she hadn't even realized was trying to conceive. Not having that context made it impossible for Misty to step up for Kerri in the way she would have wanted and ultimately changed the tenor of their bond. "That put chinks in the armor a little bit, taking it more to a business relationship than a partnership," Misty says, acknowledging the level of emotional transparency that having a certain type of work-wife bond requires. When Kerri got pregnant with her second child, the same cycle repeated itself—this time on a world stage at the London 2012 Olympics. Misty had a sneaking suspicion that Kerri was expecting during their precompetition practices, but Kerri was mum on the subject. (For the sake of clarity: We interviewed Kerri and Misty separately, and this particular issue didn't come up in our conversation with Kerri. When we shared this story with her, she remembered it differently but noted that "feelings are feelings, and that colors our memories.") Though Kerri surely had her reasons for keeping the news to herself, that left Misty feeling she couldn't be her best, most supportive self in this very clutch moment in their shared career. "Let us [our coach and me] help. As a partner, a friend, I hoped she would tell me, but what are you going to do?" Misty adds. Like it or not, Misty had to carry some of Kerri's baby weight, too—not only managing for her shifting state, but also finding an interim partner during her first pregnancy. Though increased visibility into Kerri's thinking and plans wouldn't have changed that, it could have given the two of them a chance to devise a plan that was both deliberate and collaborative.

But even the best-laid plans can't account for the emotional burden of one partner holding down the fort sans her other half. Take, for instance, the Food52 founders: After executing a successful postpartum support strategy during Merrill's first pregnancy, the birth of Merrill's second child left Amanda struggling to keep it together while leading the team on her own. "On her second maternity leave, I had a mental breakdown," Amanda says. "It was a culmination of a lot of things. It was just a lot of bad shit going on." Merrill went into labor shortly after the company had moved into a new office, where Amanda's anxieties manifested themselves in extreme attention to detail—vacuuming the entire space, sanding doorknobs, and generally overworking herself to the point where she was physically, mentally, and emotionally depleted. "I just went into this deep funk—this depression—and I went and saw Merrill. She said, 'I really think you need to talk to somebody. You're not in a good place, and I'm here to support you,'" Amanda remembers. "We both learned how to grow through some tough times. I felt like I didn't know how to function without Merrill."

The challenges of showing up for each other last long past maternity leave, and they can be especially tricky if one partner doesn't have kids. Working moms simply have fewer hours in the day to work, and when Sherry Jhawar and Allison Statter started pursuing their L.A.-based celebrity and influencer marketing agency Blended Strategy Group, that asymmetry was a given: Sherry was child-free, and Allison had recently given birth to her third son. In fact, for Allison, that new baby was part of the motivation for diving into the partnership: "I started to have reservations about going to work every day and leaving my kids for something that I didn't feel was my own. I think starting my own business was the only thing that was going to make it worth it for me." For Sherry's part, she was plenty comfortable with Allison's child-rearing status—as she says, "I love kids, and I want to be a mom myself at the right time. I have no issue with the fact that she's a working mom and the balance that needs to be struck with that." But she *was* trepidatious about what would happen if Allison was to become pregnant with her fourth child early in their work-wife tenure, leaving Sherry temporarily on her own to navigate the very insider world of entertainment as an outsider. So she raised the question of whether another kid was in the cards before the two of them even committed to joining forces. "We had that conversation, and Allison said, 'Look, I don't know. Not anytime soon. I think I'm done, but you never know,'" Sherry recalls. "I thought, 'You know what? I'm going to trust this answer of "Life is life." If something happens, then something happens, and she'd be able to roll with it.'"

Now that they're three years into their partnership, Allison is the one who is more concerned about what being a mom means for their relationship. "I think it weighs on me more than it does on Sherry, just because she has more capacity than I have, which I get really insecure about," says Allison, noting that Sherry has the highest capacity for work of anyone she's ever encountered. "I think that I actually didn't have those concerns coming into it. I have them more now just knowing how much work there is. I want to make sure I'm doing as much as she is so that she's not getting stuck and feeling rundown because she has to do more."

On Challenges and Wins

In addition to the logistical, psychological, and emotional challenges of factoring babies into the partnership, there are also real brass-tacks considerations—which the trio of lawyers behind KMR was forced to contend with early on. Imagine the height of our eyebrows and the slack of our jaws when we learned that at the time of our interview, there were *two* pregnant bellies among them. Both Keli Knight and Yondi Morris-Andrews were about to have their first babies—in Yondi's case, twins—with due dates six weeks apart. They were flooded with anxieties, including how to keep the company operating smoothly. "*We're* the fund to pay people, as business owners," Yondi says, explaining their reluctance to bring on extra hands during this time. "I know that if we were to hire someone, it means that I take home this amount less per month, and with new expenses coming on, like a nanny—and just the expenses of children—it hits double." How would their business and partnership function with two of the three of them stepping back for a bit, leaving their third partner, Jessica Reddick, flying mostly solo? "I know it'll work itself out. We all care—and this company is our baby also—so I know that we'll never compromise the business," Jessica says.

As stressful as this scenario is to navigate short-term, the good news is that being a parent can make a person a more effective and efficient partner. Same goes for being a hard-working expecting parent, even—something *Glamour* magazine's former, longtime editor in chief Cindi Leive knew well when, in 2014, she hired Giovanna Gray Lockhart to be the magazine's Washington, D.C., editor when Giovanna was eight and a half months pregnant. As Allyson Downey reports in her book, *Here's the Plan: Your Practical, Tactical Guide to Advancing Your Career During Pregnancy and Parenthood,* when Giovanna came back to work after maternity leave, she thanked Cindi for taking a chance on her. Cindi didn't see it that way at all. Instead, she recognized that pregnancy brings out a host of vulnerabilities—physical, professional, all of them—and that someone who would push through them to apply for a job a few weeks before giving birth has ambition in spades. "Those are the type of people I want on my team," Cindi said.

With that in mind, understanding the positive effects that becoming a parent can have on a person's work is critical. With thirty years in the field of leadership development, Marian N. Ruderman, the research director at the Center for Creative Leadership, was skeptical about the widespread notion that being a working parent is bad for business. "I did not believe the results out there about how depleting it is to have a full life," she told *Forbes*. Along with some of her colleagues, Marian looked at family role commitment (i.e., responsibility to a partner or kids) in 347 managers and executives, interviewing their employees, bosses, and coworkers about their performance. Turns out that just having kids doesn't make someone a stronger manager, but being actively involved in raising them does. Managers who were committed to family life got much better reviews than their completely work-focused peers. The study pointed to a whole host of benefits, from practice at multitasking to enriched interpersonal skills, that come from trying to wrangle a toddler into a car seat while taking a work call.

This is something those who have mommed before seem to just feel in their bones, and that understanding was especially striking in the two pairs of cross-generational partners we had the privilege of sitting down with. Take Hexima: "I told Marilyn [about my pregnancy] before I accepted the CEO position just to make sure that she didn't think it was inappropriate," Nicole recalls. Hearing that news, Marilyn expressed delight, not misgivings, and supported bringing Nicole's big reveal to the board. For Deborah Jackson of Plum Alley, who raised two now-grown daughters before going into business with Andrea Turner Moffitt, who was still deep in the potty-training and *Paw Patrol* stages, the newish parent aspect felt like a win. Deborah came at this relationship with the hard-earned wisdom that nobody gets it done quite like a working mom. "I've been there myself. I worked through having two kids and all of that, and I know how unbelievably hard it is, but it doesn't bother me. In fact, I think women that have children are *just as* committed, and they're often even more efficient. Andrea does not mess around," Deborah says. "You have kids or not—it does not matter—you still work it out somehow."

For all our own anxieties around what such a transition could look like, we found comfort in talking to so many work wives who have made the motherhood leap in one form or another—especially magazine savants Kim France and Andrea Linett, who experienced what it was like to introduce parenthood into their very established bond. Andrea had Baby Gino a few years after she and Kim left *Lucky* magazine, but Kim still had a good deal of unease about how it would impact their dynamic when Andrea became a mama. "It hasn't changed her, and I was very worried that it was going to change the nature of our relationship," says Aunt Kim as the four of us gush over a photo of her and Gino. "He was three weeks old, and Andrea was like, 'I've got to get out of the fucking house.' She is still the same."

We think we'll be the same, too—the same women who worry plenty about change but who also feel empowered to shape their own lives and workplaces. Office culture was constructed by men who, for the most part, saw parenting as a weekend hobby (looking at you, Don Draper), but that's shifting as our society gets its head in the game—and as work wives like us take over. Having the privilege to take matters into our own hands, for ourselves and those in our professional orbit, is what will change the workplace and, fingers crossed, the world.

Making Way for Matriarchy

We're women. We have a double standard
to live up to.

—ALLY McBEAL, *ALLY McBEAL*

Having a work wife requires courage. You have to be willing to feel exposed. You have to be open to being *this close* to someone when things get dark—or, possibly, go dark. You have to be willing to communicate and to express your feelings and to continually strive to get better at both. You have to learn to get angry in a productive way. You have to be down with being so wrapped up in another person's well-being— a person with whom you exchanged no vows but maybe should have—that you acknowledge her to be, as Kerri Walsh Jennings puts it, the yin to your yang.

More than anything, you have to be willing to be human. In a 2012 commencement speech, Sheryl Sandberg advised an audience of Harvard Business School graduates, "Bring your whole self to work." She continued: "I don't believe we have a professional self Monday through Friday and a real self the rest of the time. It is all professional, and it is all personal." Feminist theory has long held that men, by insisting on clear boundaries between domestic and office life, have strategically and fundamentally limited the ways in which women can succeed in the workplace. Take, for example, pregnancy and breastfeeding: If these acts are sequestered to the personal, new and expecting mothers will have a hell of a time proving their professional potential. (A pregnant belly is a remarkably hard thing to leave at home.) So, then, what better way to resist this systematic oppression than to bring something that is not only deeply personal but also distinctly nuanced and exclusive to women—our relationships—to business?

This also just makes good practical sense: There are fewer and fewer jobs in the world that allow for a clear delineation between work and life. Courtney E. Martin writes, "You don't have a work *slash* life; you do work that is interwoven into the larger context of your life." We Snapchat with our bosses; we work at all hours—and sometimes from home. It also goes the other way: We talk about hiring decisions over manicures. We update one another on newsletter campaigns while we wait for a friend to show up for drinks. We share links to articles and photos of nephews in the same breath as we ask, "Did you get a chance to look at that new web design?" The work-wife relationship gets to the heart of this work-life mash-up that we all, for better or worse, increasingly have to reckon with. If done right, it's a way to achieve at least a small sem-blance of balance—to have a lot of things, since, as it turns out, we can't have it all. By virtue of the presence of another human to laugh, cry, and laugh-cry with, we get pleasure and leisure—and comfort and emotional support—in an always-on-the-clock climate.

Learning to get so very real with one woman creates a pat-tern of behavior that echoes across interactions with other women, too. In time, as this way of being moves from duos and trios to larger swaths of women, it can reshape the dy-namics of a male-centric workplace or industry from within. One anecdote that came up frequently during our interviews and research was the story of female staffers at the Obama White House who joined forces to get their voices heard. In the early days of the administration, men ruled the roost—two thirds of Obama's top aides were male—so in order to bubble up their ideas in meetings—and to make sure they ac-tually got credit for them before some guy claimed them as his own—women would amplify what another woman had said, repeating her thought and attaching her name to it (e.g., "I think it's worth exploring the idea that so-and-so shared."). This simple behavioral change led to real progress: During the second term, there was gender parity among those with close proximity to POTUS. As bands of women come together and into their own, they create a network effect, giving us a glimpse into what a matriarchal work culture could look like and how it would diverge from—and remake—the patriarchal one that is all we've known. How would meetings be run, goals set, and successes determined? How would offices feel and corporations function? What would all of our lives look like as a result?

Marginalized groups throughout history have relied on strength in numbers to make change, and coalitions of women have power—whether they're formally structured or more loosely bonded, as in the case of 1850s suffragists (shout-out to OG work wives Susan B. Anthony and Elizabeth Cady Stanton), Harvey Weinstein's sexual assault accusers, Women's March organizers, or professional athletes, like the tennis stars who came together to fight for equal pay in the seventies or, more recently, the WNBA players who boycotted after being fined for wearing Black Lives Matter shirts. This idea in no way discounts the fierceness of one woman on her own—but it does underscore the fact that women's proclivity for partnership and collaboration has been, and will continue to be, a catalyst for systemic change.

Work-wifing begets broad progress and also personal growth. It is undeniably hard to be a woman who wants to make shit happen. A woman, period. Experiencing that struggle so intimately alongside another person has been one of the most rewarding experiences of our adult lives. As we evolve—as managers, employees, friends, wives, daughters, grown-ups, citizens—we look to each other for support, accountability, guidance, and, sometimes, to be a full-on compass. And here's the other win: Being a duo—or trio or quartet—of women is fun. Let's not forget that part. We highly recommend it—four very enthusiastic thumbs up.

Acknowledgments

Thank you to the women who sat down with us to share their experiences as work wives and whose kindness, generosity, and vulnerability made those sessions feel more like therapy than interviews.

To the women who have fought for our rights and opportunities in the workplace and the ones who continue to do so.

To our families, and especially our parents, Barb and Greg Cerulo and Barbara and Steve Mazur, who have exhibited boundless confidence in us, who have handed out our business cards even when we've wished they hadn't, and who have gotten vanity license plates in celebration of our accomplishments.

To our husbands, Thomas Hauner and Chris Roan, who have welcomed a third into their marriages and have never once complained that they had no choice in the matter. Their unpaid labor is the stuff of feminist fantasies. We both love you both.

To the University of Chicago, for teaching us how to think and for finally putting us in the alumni magazine.

To Rush Atkinson, who set us up on our first friend date and is definitely worth an internet search.

To the people who have gone to bat for us and our business beyond any reasonable expectations—many before we really had a business to speak of: Alice Akawie, Anna Akawie, Shirley Akawie, David Aronoff, Jamie Beck, Melissa Coker, Mandy Coon, Chelsa Crowley, Lorry Dudley, Jessy Fofana, Kathryn Fortunato, Lizzie Fortunato, Sarah Fox, Jeremy Goldstein, Lindsey Green, Andy Hamingson, Julia Hunter, Kevin Kearney, Courtney Klein, Glynnis MacNicol, Frank Manheim, Joe Martinez, Ken McVay, Ben Michaelis, Andrea Oliveri, Kate Oppenheim, Anthony Pergola, Dan Refai, Will Schenk, Ben Schippers, Craig Shapiro, Rachel Sklar, Matt Singer, Rex Sorgatz, Elizabeth Spiers, Steve Spurgat, Max Stein, David Sunberg, Orest Tomaselli, Ellen Van Dusen, Cary Vaughan, Nicole Vecchiarelli, Clare Vivier, Erica Weiner, Jenna Wilson, Joanne Wilson, and Amy Ziskin.

To our champions at Bed Bath & Beyond, for your belief in us, for your incredible support, and for 20 percent off all our purchases: Jason Bernstein, Warren Eisenberg, Leonard Feinstein, Scott Hames, Eric Steinberger, and Steven Temares.

To our employees, past and present, for putting forty (or sixty or eighty) hours a week into realizing this vision alongside us: Joan Baker, Grace Canlas, Michelle Gattenio, Rachel Herzig, Marie Joh, Susie Lee, Sally Nadeau, Jessie Newland, Melanie Sellinger, Liz Sheldon, Colin Smight, Katherin Son, Keely Thomas-Menter, and Ruby Tucker.

To every last one of our interns, who have taught us so much and left us with very good stories.

To our editor, Sara Weiss, who believed we had a book in us *way* before we did, Elana Seplow-Jolley, and the whole Ballantine team for bringing this book to life.

To our agent, Kari Stuart, for being our advocate and cheerleader and for very much getting that work-wife lifestyle, as well as Cat Shook and the entire ICM team.

To Alex Ronan, whose good research—and enthusiasm—made this book so much better.

To Courtney Martin, whose work inspired us to go down this road and whose feedback and stamp of approval helps us sleep at night.

To our friends, who put up with a lot (and many of them from both of us): Britt Aboutaleb, Ruthie Baron, Eliza Bent, Brianna Corrado, Amanda Dobbins, Tania Fogg, Dan Frommer, Jess Iannotti, Bryce Jones, Kelsey Jones, Christine Kim, Bridget Lademann, Adam Laukhuf, Marisa Meltzer, Keri Morelock, Laura Neilson, Yaran Noti, Priya Rao, Kayleen Schaefer, Lauren Sherman, Candace Smith, Aminatou Sow, Katie Sutcliffe, and Paige Sweet.

Sources

The following are books that we reference and quote in the preceding pages:

- *The Founder's Dilemmas: Anticipating and Avoiding the Pitfalls That Can Sink a Startup* by Noam Wasserman (pp. 34–35)
- *Here's the Plan: Your Practical, Tactical Guide to Advancing Your Career During Pregnancy and Parenthood* by Allyson Downey (p. 176)
- *Mating in Captivity: Unlocking Erotic Intelligence* by Esther Perel (p. 89)

- *The New Better Off: Reinventing the American Dream* by Courtney E. Martin (pp. 91, 103, 181)
- *Wellbeing: The Five Essential Elements* by Tom Rath and Jim Harter (pp. 78–79)
- *You're the Only One I Can Tell: Inside the Language of Women's Friendships* by Deborah Tannen (pp. 71–72, 153)

We also cite various studies, surveys, and articles that are highly googleable, for all you primary source enthusiasts.

Additionally, these three books have informed our approach and thinking on the topics we address:

- *Making Ideas Happen: Overcoming the Obstacles Between Vision and Reality* by Scott Belsky
- *Small Giants: Companies That Choose to Be Great Instead of Big* by Bo Burlingham
- *Text Me When You Get Home: The Evolution and Triumph of Modern Female Friendship* by Kayleen Schaefer

For Nicole Kidman's 2017 Emmy acceptance speech that reflects on her professional and personal relationship with Reese Witherspoon, Maya Angelou's 1997 advice to Oprah on *The Oprah Winfrey Show,* and Sheryl Sandberg's 2012 Harvard Business School commencement speech, get yourself to YouTube.

About the Authors

ERICA CERULO and CLAIRE MAZUR met as undergrads at the University of Chicago in 2002 and founded Of a Kind in 2010. They have developed a reputation as influential curators at the forefront of the maker movement, with a knack for identifying "the next big thing" when it's still a small thing. In addition to unearthing America's most talented up-and-coming designers for features on their website, Mazur and Cerulo have also become known for their popular *10 Things* newsletter and its podcast companion A Few Things, where they expand their enthusiasm for new discoveries across product and lifestyle categories. Accolades for Cerulo and Mazur have included being named to *Forbes*'s "30 Under 30," *InStyle*'s "Best of the Web," and *Fashionista*'s "Most Influential People in New York Fashion Right Now." This is their first book.

ofakind.com
@ericacerulo / @clairemazur / @workwifehq / @ofakind

About the Type

This book was set in Sabon, a typeface designed by the well-known German typographer Jan Tschichold (1902–74). Sabon's design is based upon the original letter forms of sixteenth-century French type designer Claude Garamond and was created specifically to be used for three sources: foundry type for hand composition, Linotype, and Monotype. Tschichold named his typeface for the famous Frankfurt typefounder Jacques Sabon (c. 1520–80).